THE PRACTITIONER'S GUIDE TO PROJECT MANAGEMENT

The Practitioner's Guide to

PROJECT MANAGEMENT

Simple, Effective Techniques that Deliver Business Value

LYNDA CARTER

Foreword by Gary Slavin
Illustrated by David Balan

Competitive Edge Consulting, Inc., Cleveland 44107
©2014 by Lynda Carter
Printed in the United States of America

ISBN: 978-0-9903549-0-1 (hardcover)
ISBN: 978-0-9903549-1-8 (paperback)
ISBN: 978-0-9903549-2-5 (e-book)

Library of Congress Control Number: 2014913047

Edited by Brenda Judy
www.publishersplanet.com

Illustrated by David Balan
www.davidbalan.com

Cover and Interior Design by Carolyn Sheltraw
www.csheltraw.com

∞ This paper meets the requirements of ANSI/NISO Z39.48-1992 (Permanence of Paper).

www.cectraining.com

To my family for all their love and encouragement:
Mark, Rachel, Nicole, and Yvonne too!

Table of Contents

Foreword

I first met Lynda Carter several years ago while working on a project with her. From the onset, I was impressed with her understanding of project management and her rare ability to communicate in a way that enabled everyone to understand the goals of a project and stay motivated to work together to achieve success. We have since collaborated on a couple other projects, and I have always enjoyed working with and learning from someone with a tremendous grasp on the ins and outs of project management.

Project management is the process and activity of planning, organizing, motivating and controlling resources, procedures and protocols to achieve specific goals in scientific or daily problems. It was practiced informally for many years, but began to emerge as a distinct profession in the mid-twentieth century. Now, project management is almost a buzz word and well-practiced in most, if not all, major corporations around the world. This, in turn, has led to a proliferation of project management books and courses.

Why then do we need yet another book on this subject? Well, Lynda Carter has come up with a unique, very interesting and easy-to-read illustrative guide to project management that you won't find in any library, bookstore or obtain from any learning institution. Lynda's goal was to create a guide that could be used as a textbook in any learning institution as well as a self-paced guide for any level of practitioner. The pages of this book contain timeless lessons on how best to apply the rules and processes of project management that she has refined over the years. I'm sure you will find this book to be both educational and an invaluable resource.

I have been practicing and conducting training on project management for over thirty years, and this is the first book on the subject that I was able to read from cover to cover and still be awake upon finishing. I found Lynda's writing to be entertaining and informative, which is a very rare quality for any book covering material of this nature. *The Practitioner's Guide to Project Management: Simple, Effective Techniques that Deliver Business Value* is the most comprehensive book I've read on project management. Lynda Carter's writing style makes you feel as if you are standing side-by-side with her as she walks you through the steps required to ensure your project is a success and delivers a product that exceeds your sponsor's expectations.

So, prepare yourself to journey with Lynda though the trials and tribulations of an experienced project manager, and don't be surprised if you're entertained while learning some valuable techniques that you will be able to utilize to ensure your current and future projects are completed successfully.

Gary Slavin
Trainer, Consultant and Author of
Plan Your Success: Turn Your Dreams Into Reality
www.garyslavin.com

Acknowledgments

I never really appreciated the value and contributions of those that are acknowledged in books; but now I do. This book is an accumulation of years of experience; for that I am thankful to all the clients that have invited me into their organizations to assist them in their pursuit of improved project management. I am grateful to teach at a university that supports my passion, and for the students that used the first draft of this book for their supplemental reading.

I am thankful for Gary Slavin's relentless pursuit of my writing. Gary's endless e-mails of encouragement and recommendations transformed my book writing endeavors from bucket list to realization. Thank you, Gary.

I am grateful to have worked with Brenda Judy, my editor, who poured over every word, over and over, to ensure my thoughts make sense on paper, as well as Carolyn Sheltraw, who designed the book cover and formatted my words and graphics.

I am thankful for the individuals that have been great teachers to me, many of them are clients that over the years have turned into great colleagues and friends; they include: Carrie Brainerd, Pete Evangelista, Gerri Huri, Dr. Harold Kerzner, Gary Livingston, Mary Jean Milanko, Pat Ray, Ted Russell, Sue Russell (no relation to Ted), Mary Schwendeman, Mary Sutcliffe, Donna VanRooy, Jeff Young and Bethann Zavenson.

To all of you that have been part of my journey, whom I did not mention here, my sincere apologies.

Author's Introduction

Hello, I am Lynda Carter; let me begin by introducing myself. I began my career in software development, back in the days when a mainframe was the only available option (so it was a long time ago). I ran software development and process improvement projects by the seat of my pants, and loved what I was doing.

In 1992, I had the opportunity to leave the corporate world and begin a consulting career. I had a great business partner, and the adventure began. Since then, I have been building custom training solutions, facilitating meetings and workshops, creating project management curriculum, starting and organizing Project Management Offices (PMOs), lending my expertise to executives who want to embrace project management, coaching project and program managers, and assisting organizations in assessing their organizational maturity in project management. I also teach Project Management at the undergraduate and graduate levels at Baldwin Wallace University.

Baldwin Wallace University is known as a center of excellence in project management in great part because Dr. Harold Kerzner—a prolific author, lecturer and the authoritative voice of best practices in project management—spent many years teaching there. I have taken classes from Dr. Kerzner and have been fortunate enough to work with him.

Over the years, I have seen project management applications that drive organizations' success and, unfortunately, some that create documentation-driven bureaucracies.

It is my desire to share simple, effective project management techniques in a way that encourages collaborative conversations with key resources and delivers business value.

I hope you find this enhances your journey for a more effective application of project management.

Good luck, have fun and embrace what drives your success.

About the Illustrator

David Balan is a recent graduate from the Savannah College of Art and Design. He is an accomplished cartoonist with multiple awards and honors from his undergraduate studies, including an international exhibition in Lacoste, France. His senior project, a collaborative pitch for a graphic novel, *Steelfoot Fin and the Last Oil Well*, was featured in a solo exhibition at the Muse Gallery in Longmont, Colorado. Since graduating, he has worked with Random House Inc. and the Cleveland Museum of Contemporary Art on projects for both digital and traditional publication.

David is also passionate about education. He was a certified Peer Tutor during his last year of college, and since has volunteered for multiple art education workshops and seminars. Some of his workshops include Moleskine Words at Utrecht Art Supplies in Savanah, Georgia, Superhero Art Camp at the Ohio State University, and the Mosaic Project Comics Workshop at Fairview High School.

The Practitioner's Guide to Project Management marks David's first long-format illustration project—an undertaking with both art and education at its focus. He's had a blast helping illuminate the subject with his cartoons, and he hopes you'll find learning about project management just as enjoyable!

Section 1:

PROJECT MANAGEMENT OVERVIEW

This section provides an executive summary of the book, containing an introduction of the basic project management concepts and detailing the standard project lifecycle.

Chapter 1: Introduction

Chapter 1 will help you understand what project management is through an introduction to the project management lifecycle; a description of project management deliverables; an introduction to the standard topics, questions and techniques used in project management; common project trade-offs; and common questions about project management.

Let's start by answering a few questions about projects and project management:

What is a project?

> Anytime you do something new, something unique, where you need to get organized and determine the best strategy to get something done, you have a project.

How big is a project?

> Projects vary in size and complexity; they can be:

> Small – lasting a brief amount of time (days, weeks or a few months) and requiring a small team (or maybe only one person).

Large – taking a significant amount of time (possibly multiple years) and many resources. Super large projects are often called Programs. Programs are a group of related projects managed and coordinated to obtain benefits not available from individual projects.

Medium – anywhere between small and large.

What is project management?

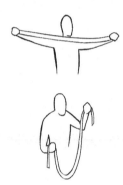

Project management is a structured, yet flexible approach to apply standardized tools and techniques in order to increase the likelihood that your project will be planned and executed successfully. There are two major institutions that globally support the project management discipline: The Project Management Institute (PMI) from the United States and Prince2 from the United Kingdom.

When should I use project management?

Whenever you have a project (unique idea to achieve), use project management. There are many project management tools and techniques. Not every tool or technique should be used on all projects. The purpose of project management is to drive project success, not to fill out a series of forms and documents. So, when planning your project, think, "Will this tool help the project succeed?" If the answer is yes, use the tool; if not, keep the tool aside for use at another time.

Who are the players involved in projects?

There are formal roles in project management. Each role will be detailed later in the text. For an introduction, here are the key roles that you should find on any project:

Icon	Role and Primary Responsibility
	The **Sponsor** is *or* represents the primary project benefactor, and sets the overall project direction.
	The **Project Manager** is responsible for facilitating the project planning execution and closing while providing leadership to the project team.
	The **project team** supports the Project Manager and completes project work.
	The **Subject Matter Expert** (SME) provides expertise on project strategy and project-related information.
	The **Stakeholder** is anyone who is actively involved in the project or impacted by the execution or completion of the project.

Now that you have a common understanding of what project management is, let's define the concept of a project lifecycle.

Project Lifecycle

All projects go through a standard lifecycle that begins as an idea, requires planning, then consumes time and resources in project execution, and finally ends in reflective learning for the benefit of future projects.

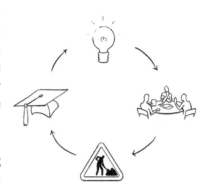

Let's begin by briefly reviewing each lifecycle stage, description and output:

Icon	Formally Known as	Description	Output
	Idea/Need/ Problem **Initiation**	When an idea or need is identified, the first step (phase or stage) is to clarify what the idea is, and develop a high-level best guess of what work, resources and time it will take to bring the idea to reality	• Project Charter • Business Case • Decision to stop or move forward with project planning

Icon	Formally Known as	Description	Output
	Plan **Planning**	Collaborative creation of the detailed strategy needed to achieve the approved project goals, which is created under the direction of a Project Manager	• Detailed Project Plan • Decision to stop, or move forward and support the detailed project strategy
	Execute the Plan **Execution**	Getting the work done; following the Project Plan; managing resources, issues, risks and changes; and preparing progress status reports	• Updated Project Plan • Project Deliverables • Project Status Reports
	Knowledge Capture and Learning **Closing**	Formally closing out the project, and capturing project learnings to improve the strategies used in future projects	• Lessons Learned • Final Updated Project Plan • Project Evaluation

Project Management Deliverables

A deliverable is something tangible that is created as a result of the project. There are two basic types of deliverables:

- Project management deliverables – items created for the management of a formal project
- Project deliverables – items created to achieve the project goals

For now, we'll only be discussing the standard documents that are created to manage the project, which are the "project management deliverables." Each document fulfills a unique purpose. The following is a brief narrative describing the purpose of the key project management documents that are created and updated throughout the life of the project. More detailed information is provided in Chapter 2: Project Lifecycle Detailed.

Business Case: The Business Case is the business justification for the project. It focuses on value added to the business. Components of the Business Case are similar to the Project Charter and Project Plan, plus the all-in costs and benefits to the organization.

Project Charter (aka Initial Project Plan or Feasibility Study): The Project Charter transitions an idea into a project. The Charter documents the common understanding of the project need and high-level project strategy. It should be created collaboratively with the Project Manager and business (Project Sponsor). The Project Charter is intended to be used by the business or Project Sponsor to determine if the project has enough merit to be planned.

Project Plan (aka Statement of Work [SOW]): The Project Plan is a living, breathing, evergreen document; meaning that the Project Plan is not complete until the project is complete. Do not expect perfection, or a 100-percent accurate Project Plan, until you are close to the end of the project (or your planning team has amazingly accurate insight). The Project Plan documents the detailed project strategy.

Project Status Reports: The status report should be targeted to the unique information needs of the Sponsor. The purpose of the Status Report is to help the Sponsor and Stakeholders understand the current progress of the project.

Lessons Learned: This document captures the knowledge that was acquired during the project from the perspectives of the Sponsor, Stakeholders, Project Manager and project team members. This knowledge capture can be related to how project management was applied to the project, how the team worked together and communicated to each other, as well as technical knowledge gathered from creating the project deliverables. It is import-ant that this knowledge be shared with the project team and others in the organization to leverage lessons learned for other projects.

Project Evaluation: This document provides an overall summary of the project, and is a good go-to document for someone who wants to understand the project without investing a lot of time and digging into all the details of the project management documents. The Project Evaluation provides a summary of the project, assesses the project's actual performance versus the planned performance, and highlights key improvements that can be leveraged for future projects.

Project Management Topics and Standard Techniques

Everyone uses project management. Even individuals with no formal education or experience create plans and achieve goals; yet, there are standard techniques. These techniques ensure that you are asking the right questions and gathering the necessary information to successfully plan and execute a project.

The following is an introduction to each project management topic and the questions they help answer. Each topic has techniques that can be used to answer the questions that need to be answered. The topics, questions and related techniques are discussed in detail in Chapters 3–14.

Icon	Topic and Chapter	Questions
	Goals Chapter 3	• What will the project achieve? • What does success look like? • How will we know when we are done?

Icon	Topic and Chapter	Questions
	Stakeholders Chapter 4	• Who will be impacted? • What are their expectations? • How engaged are they in the project? • How important are they to the project? • How does the project satisfy their needs?
	Knowledge Chapter5	• What do you already know that will help drive project success? • What have you learned that will drive future success?

	Deliverables
	
	Chapter 6
		• What needs to be built/created/delivered:
		  ○ At the end of the project?
		  ○ During the life of the project?
		  ○ To manage the project?

	Quality Chapter 7	• How will you ensure that the project deliverables will meet Stakeholder expectations?
	Work Chapter 8	• What work needs to be done? • How long will the work take? • What skills are needed? • How many resources (people, materials, facilities) do you need to complete the work?

Icon	Topic and Chapter	Questions
	Project Team Chapter 9	• Does everyone understand their project role? • How will you build a positive team?
	Risks Chapter 10	• How much uncertainty is okay? • How will uncertainty be handled?
	Timing Chapter 11	• How long will the project take?
	Communication Chapter 12	• Who needs information on the project? • What do they need to know? • When do they need information? • How will they get the information?
	Financing Chapter 13	• What needs to be purchased? • What will the project cost?

	Project Execution
	
	Chapter 14
		• How will issues and changes be managed?
		• Is the project:
		  o On time?
		  o On budget?
		  o Delivering the project scope?

Terminology: The term "scope" is used in projects to define what will and will not be included in the project. Defining and documenting scope includes the following techniques from the table: goals, deliverables, quality and work. Specifically, project scope documents what the project will achieve (Goal), what the project will deliver (Deliverables), how you will know the deliverables will meet Stakeholder expectations (Quality) and the work necessary to create each deliverable (Work).

The illustration used in this text for scope is a fence with a gate. The fence is to clearly define what is in scope, and the gate is to provide someone with the authority to add or remove items from the project scope.

Project Trade-Offs

Have you ever heard the statement, "*Fast, Good and Cheap—you can only pick two*"? This statement is about trade-offs. If you want something good and fast, it will probably not be cheap; if you want something cheap and good, it might not be fast; and if you want something fast and cheap, it is not likely to be good. Fortunately, exceptions can be found to any rule. In project management, we call these trade-offs "project constraints."

All projects have constraints that will impact the project strategy. Common project constraints include:

- Time to finish the project (fast)
- Funding to support the project work (cheap)
- What the project will produce— often labeled as requirements, quality, performance or scope (good)

These constraints are often illustrated in a triangle.

Additional constraints include:

- Resources dedicated to work on the project, such as people, facilities, equipment and raw materials
- Amount of risk (uncertainty) tolerated by the organization
- Corporate political environment
- Value or image to be created or maintained

Why Understanding Constraints is Important

When planning your project, it is important to understand, from the business perspective, the priorities of these project constraints. You will make different decisions in planning the project if finishing quickly is more important than how much money is spent, or if the output/outcome of the project is more important than how much time you have to complete the project. It is not unusual to have two priority constraints. It is important that the Project Manager has some control over one of the constraints so that trade-offs in planning can be made.

Common Project Management Questions

Here are a few common questions about how project management may impact the life of an organization.

If my organization is already using a lifecycle, do I still need project management?

Many organizations have product development lifecycles in place. For example:

- software development lifecycle (SDLC)
- marketing lifecycle
- new product development lifecycle
- Define, Measure, Analyze, Improve, Control (DMAIC process improvement using Six Sigma methodology)

These lifecycles may already have components of project management imbedded in them; yet, these lifecycles are mainly focused on the product they are developing rather than on project management. So, even with other lifecycles in place, it is valuable to understand project management, and include those project management tools and techniques that will help drive the project success of whatever you are creating.

What is a PMO?

A Project (or Program) Management Office (PMO) is a function within an organization dedicated to the support of project management. There is no standard design of a PMO. Many PMOs provide support through: training, coaching, standards (forms and templates), governance and methodology.

PMOs can be developed to service a specific business function (e.g., Information Technology [IT], Marketing, Research and Development [R&D]) or a specific customer, or can be designed to support only high-visibility, high-risk projects that meet specific financial thresholds. PMOs can be permanent organizational structures or can be set up as a temporary office to support strategic objectives.

What is project management maturity?

Some organizations assess the level of project management application within their organization. The concept of maturity in a process is based on the Software Engineering Institute's (SEI) Capability Maturity Model Integration (CMMI).

The CMMI model provides a standard for which many processes can be assessed. The five levels of maturity based on the CMMI model are:

- Level 1: Common Language – sporadic use of project management, lip service or no consistent support of projects; and decisions are made based on personal preference

- Level 2: Common Process – benefits of project management are known, project management is actively supported, project management processes are followed, and a project management curriculum and career path are present

- Level 3: Singular Methodology – streamlining multiple processes into one, active management support, project management is integrated into the corporate culture and there is recognition for the specific behaviors that drive project success

- Level 4: Benchmarking – dedication to benchmarking, internally and externally

- Level 5: Continuous Improvement – dedication to lessons learned, knowledge capture, mentoring future Project Managers and continuous improvement to project management processes

Many consulting firms have created their own project management assessments, and provide as a service, for a fee, a numerical rating of an organization's level of project management maturity.

Chapter Summary

This chapter provided an introduction into the foundational elements of project management and a standard understanding of common project management terminology.

Project Management is a set of tools and techniques that can help you get organized in managing your project. There are standard tools that will assist you in managing any project: goals, stakeholders, knowledge, deliverables, quality, work, financing, risks, communications and the project team.

Standard roles in project management include: Sponsor, Stakeholder, Project Manager, SME and the project team.

All projects have constraints that will impact the project strategy. Common project constraints include:

- Time to finish the project (fast)
- Funding to support the project work (cheap)
- What the project will produce— often labeled as requirements, quality, performance or scope (good)

Projects go through a standard lifecycle, producing standard project management deliverables:

- Initiation – Business Case and Project Charter
- Planning – Project Plan
- Execution – Status Reports
- Closing – Lessons Learned and Project Evaluation

Chapter 2: Project Lifecycle Detailed

This chapter details the project management lifecycle as a series of interdependent phases or stages. Each project management stage is dependent on the output of the previous stage. The stages are interdependent but not necessarily linear (or sequential).

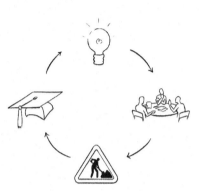

For each stage, the following items will be reviewed:

- Stage purpose, inputs and outputs
- A detailed outline of each project management deliverable
- Key roles and responsibilities
- A standard approach for work completed in the stage
- Key questions answered in the stage
- Common questions asked about the stage

Initiation (Idea/Need/Problem)

Initiation Key Components

Purpose: Formally transition from an idea to a project, and create a "good enough" estimate of the project strategy to decide if the project should be planned in detail

Input: Business Case (optional) or Business Need

Output: Project Charter, updated Business Case (optional), and decision to continue to Planning or cancel the project

The Project Charter transitions an idea into a project. The Charter documents the common understanding of the project need and high-level project strategy. It should be created collaboratively with the Project Manager and business (Project Sponsor). The Project Charter is intended to be used by the business or Project Sponsor to determine if the project has enough merit to be planned.

Project Charter, Initial Project Plan and Feasibility Study are different names given to similar documents; throughout this book, we will use the title Project Charter. Check with your organization to find out what document titles are used.

The Project Charter's primary purpose is to document a common understanding of the project and the high-level project strategy to make a business decision on whether or not to continue planning.

The Project Charter is drafted only once. There is no need to keep the Project Charter up to date throughout the life of the project. The Charter's purpose is to define the project and provide enough information to decide if Project Planning should be staffed. Once the project is defined and the decision is made, the Project Charter has served its purpose, and it can be archived until the end of the project.

The **Project Charter** should contain the following topics:

- Business Need – brief narrative detailing why the project is being pursued
- Stakeholders – list of stakeholders and their success criteria (or Key Performance Indicators)
- Preliminary Project Scope:
  - Project Goal – brief statement of what the project will achieve
  - Deliverables – final project deliverables
- High-level Risk – key events that could impact project success, and strategies for managing them
- High-level Timing – key milestones and project completion
- Key Resources – key project team members
- High-level Cost – estimated budget for project expenditures

The **Business Case** is the business justification for the project. It focuses on added value to the business. Components of the Business Case are similar to the Project Charter and Project Plan, but focused on not just the project work, but the all-in costs and benefits to the organization.

Common components of the Business Case include:

- Business Need – prioritized business goals and success criteria
- Business Strategy – how the business need will be filled—that can include marketing analysis, pricing strategies, funding approaches and other business considerations
- Results Metrics – how success will be measured
- Financial Justification – cost/benefit analysis that can include calculations for net present value, return on investment and break-even requirements

Initiation Roles and Responsibilities

Icon	Project Role	Initiation Responsibility
	Sponsor	Provides business perspective of project need and priority; defines project success criteria; reviews the Project Charter and determines if the project should proceed to Planning
	Stakeholders	Share high-level business needs from their unique perspective
	Project Manager	Works with Sponsor to define high-level project approach and creates Project Charter documentation
	Subject Matter Experts	Provide expertise based on past projects and organizational experience

The Approach to Initiation

The duration of Initiation is the briefest stage in the project lifecycle. This stage can range from a brief conversation, followed by time for documentation, or a series of conversations and a collaborative creation of the Project Charter.

Initiation is a one-time event.

Common mistakes that occur in the Initiation stage and Project Charter creation include:

- Assuming that the estimates from Initiation are accurate (they are rough guesses, given the limited information known)
- Not including the Project Manager or a Subject Matter Expert (SME) in drafting the Project Charter
- Holding the Project Manager accountable in project execution for meeting performance, completion dates and funding targets set in the Initiation stage

Key Questions Answered in the Initiation Stage

 During the Initiation stage, a few of the project management tools and techniques are applied to create a common vision of the project approach, and answer the following questions:

Questions	What the Answer will Provide
What will the project achieve?	• Business need • Success criteria for each stakeholder • Preliminary project scope (project goals and final deliverables)
How long will the project take?	• High-level estimate of major deliverable completion and project completion
What will the project cost?	• High-level cost
Can the project be successful?	• High-level risk and key resources • Enough information that the decision makers agree with the project strategy, that key staffing is available and that the project has enough priority within the organization to move to Planning

Common Questions About Initiation

Who is responsible for leading the Initiation stage?

> In many organizations, the Project Manager is not involved during the Initiation stage of a project. In these cases, the business or Project Sponsor may draft the Project Charter—hopefully, with the help of a SME.

> When no Project Manager is assigned, this stage is often skipped; therefore, the Project Manager must gather both Initiation and Planning information during the Planning stage.

> If a Project Manager is assigned, then the Project Manager will facilitate the charting process and potentially create the Project Charter. A majority of the information gathered in the Initiation stage will come from collaboration between the business and the Project Manager or SME.

How much time should the Initiation stage take?

> This is the briefest stage of the project lifecycle. It should take only a small percentage of the total time dedicated to the project.

> Some organizations set standards for the amount of effort that can be spent in Initiation. One organization may use the rule of no more than forty hours of combined effort, while another organization may demand no more than eight hours of duration. These guidelines need to take into consideration the complexity and amount of information needed before your organization can make a decision to move forward to Planning, or cancel the project.

Does the Project Charter need updating throughout the life of the project?

No, updates to the Project Charter are not necessary. The Project Charter can be archived once a decision is made to move to Project Planning or to cancel the project. Archiving is necessary so that the Project Charter can be leveraged for future projects and reflected on during project Closing.

What does saying "yes" to the Project Charter mean?

A yes to the Charter means that the organization and the Project Sponsor agree to staff and fund the Project Planning stage. A yes to the Project Charter is *not* a yes to project execution.

Planning (Plan)

Planning Key Components

Purpose: Document a common vision of the project goals and agreed on strategy for achieving the project goals. The project strategy will be used to reevaluate the organization's commitment to the project and guide project execution if the project is approved

Input: Project Charter and Business Case (optional)

Output: Project Plan, updated Business Case (optional), and the organization's decision to continue, cancel or delay the project

Although the Project Plan is used for gaining commitment, it is a technical planning document intended for the Project Manager and project team. The Business Case gathers project strategy and cost information (from the Project Plan), as well as additional business information, and is intended to be used by the business or Project Sponsor.

The Business Case may be updated during the Planning stage if the information gathered during planning impacts the business justification for the project.

The Project Plan and Statement of Work (SOW) are different names for similar documents. Some organizations use SOW for contracting work when following a procurement process. Historically, the term Project Plan was a reference for only the project schedule. Now, the term Project Plan refers to the entire project plan.

For the purposes of this text, Project Plan is being used to reference either the Project Plan or SOW. Check with your organization to find out what document titles are used.

The Project Plan is a living, breathing, evergreen document; meaning that the Project Plan is not complete until the project is complete. Do not expect perfection, or a 100-percent accurate Project Plan, until you are close to the end of the project (or your planning team has amazingly accurate insight).

The **Project Plan** should contain the following topics:

- Business Need – brief narrative detailing why the project is being pursued
- Stakeholders – list of stakeholders and their success criteria (or Key Performance Indicators), and a strategy for engaging stakeholders in project execution
- Project Scope:
  - Project Goal – brief statement of what the project will achieve

- o Deliverables – interim deliverables created during the project, final deliverables turned over at the end of the project and project management deliverables used to manage the project. Each deliverable should include a brief narrative or list of acceptance criteria (also known as requirements) so that there is a common understanding of the deliverable
- o Work – the work steps necessary to create each project deliverable
- Risk – the uncertain events that could impact project success, and strategies for managing them
- Communication Strategy – how to ensure that the right information gets to the right people at the right time
- Timing – when project phases and key deliverables will be completed, and when the entire project will be completed
- Project Team – project team members, responsibilities, skill sets and level of commitment necessary to complete the project based on the project deliverables and timing
- Cost – an overall budget for project expenditures

Additional items frequently included in a Project Plan include:

- Constraints – limitations outside the project that the project is bound to perform within
- Assumptions – understandings that impact the overall project strategy

Planning Roles and Responsibilities

Icon	Project Role	Planning Responsibility
	Sponsor	Provides business perspective of project need and priority, defines project success criteria, supports the collaborative planning process, reviews Project Plan and determines if the project should proceed to Execution
	Stakeholders	Share business needs and specific expectations (Key Performance Indicators [KPI] from their unique perspective)
	Project Manager	Facilitates the planning processing and application of project management techniques, ensuring that the right individuals are engaged in collaborative planning
	SMEs and Project Team	Provide subject matter expertise based on past projects and organizational experience

The Approach to Planning

The most complete planning is done by a small collaborative team under the leadership of the Project Manager. The more knowledge and experience utilized in the creation of the Plan, the more accurate the Project Plan will be.

During Planning, the Project Manager will utilize the project management techniques necessary to define and document the Project Plan. The duration of Planning is dependent on the size and complexity of the project and the need for accuracy. If a high level of accuracy is expected as a result of planning, then the following items are necessary:

- Collaboration of SMEs and key team members in developing the Project Plan
- Historical data for actuals from similar projects
- Pilots, prototypes or tests to simulate the project on a small scale, then the actuals and lessons learned are used to complete the Project Plan for the remaining project

The Project Plan should be reviewed with the Project Sponsor and decision makers to ensure that the detailed plan is supported by leadership and that the project should move into the Execution stage.

Planning is not a one-time event. Ongoing planning and updating the Project Plan with more detailed information and approved project changes should be completed throughout the life of the project.

Workshop Idea: Holding a Project Planning Workshop

One of the best approaches to planning (and my favorite) is to hold a collaborative workshop that includes representation from the business and project team. Collaborative workshops provide a way for the entire team to create a common vision and strategy to achieve the project goal. Begin the workshop with the business (Project Sponsor) sharing the need for the project and providing a clear vision of what success at project completion looks like; then the Project Manager can facilitate the workshop by having the participants collaboratively answer the following questions:

- What have you learned in past projects that can aid in the success of this project?
- Who are the Stakeholders; and what does success look like to them?
- What work must be done to satisfy the business need and Stakeholder success criteria?
- When, across the calendar, will the work begin and end?
- What resources are needed to complete the work; and what are their roles and responsibilities?
- What uncertainty may impact the project; and what are strategies to manage the uncertainty?
- How will the team communicate and share information with Stakeholders?

Answering these questions will provide a draft Project Plan. At the end of the workshop, the Project Sponsor should review the draft Project Plan to verify that they understand and agree to the project approach. These collaborative workshops give everyone an equal voice, a forum to be heard and an opportunity to build buy-in to the overall project approach.

End the workshop with action items and next steps. The Project Manager can take the workshop output and create the necessary Project Plan documentation.

Key Questions Answered in the Planning Stage

 During the Planning stage, many of the project management tools and techniques are applied to create a common vision of the project approach and answer the following questions:

Questions	What the Answer will Provide
What will we deliver?	• Interim project deliverables • Final project deliverables • Project management deliverables • A brief narrative or list of acceptance criteria so that there is a common understanding of each deliverable
Who will be impacted?	• Stakeholders and their needed level of project engagement • Communication strategy
How will success be measured?	• Project goals • Success criteria for each Stakeholder
What work will be done?	• Work items for each deliverable
How will work be monitored?	• Project tracking strategy • Status reporting content
What resources will be needed?	• Detailed resources required for each deliverable • Skill requirements

Questions	What the Answer will Provide
What risks may occur, and how will they be managed?	• Overall project risk tolerance • Strategies for managing risks integrated into the Project Plan
What will it cost?	• Project budget
How long will the project take?	• When deliverables will be created • Amount of time project team members will be needed

Common Questions About Planning

How complete should the Project Plan be before project Execution begins?

The Project Plan should be complete enough that:

- The organization can make an informed decision to proceed, cancel or postpone the project.
- There is a common understanding of the project strategy and key milestone dates.
- There is a detailed plan of the work to be completed.

Remember that planning is ongoing. The Project Plan will not be completed until the end of the project.

Is a Project Plan document really necessary?

Planning is necessary—how you document the plan is up to you (or your organization if they have project standards). I have seen perfectly good plans documented on the back of a napkin (for a small project, on a large napkin) or on sticky notes in a project team room. When determining how to document the Project Plan, take into consideration:

- Visibility – Who needs to be able to see it?
- Access – Who needs to be able to update and harvest information from it?
- History – How will it be archived post-project so that other projects can leverage knowledge from it?

The location of team members and Stakeholders, adherence to project standards and knowledge management strategies should mandate how the Project Plan is documented.

How long should the Project Plan be?

The size and level of complexity of the project will dictate the length of the Project Plan. A Project Plan can be anywhere from a single page to hundreds of pages. Opt for as short as possible, as long as the content is clearly understood.

> Invest the necessary time it takes to make something clear, simple and concise. Mark Twain is quoted as saying, "I didn't have time to write a short letter, so I wrote a long one instead."

Should I use a standardized template for my Project Plan?

Templates can be a great way to get started in planning. Templates also create a standardized document so that all projects contain the same content and follow the same format, making it easier for Project Sponsors and team members to become familiar with the contents of the Project Plan. When creating templates, ensure that they:

- Are easy to understand and populate. People are often compelled to fill out all sections of a template, even when they have no idea what specific purpose it serves.
- Include samples and provide coaching. A completed template does not ensure a thorough plan.
- Provide opportunity for modification. Projects are unique by nature; items may need to be added or deleted from a template as one size does not always fit all when it comes to using templates for the unique needs of a specific project.

Why use a collaborative approach? Isn't the Project Manager responsible for creating the Project Plan?

The Project Manager is responsible for creating the Project Plan. The Project Manger's strategy should be to lead in the facilitation and documentation of the Project Plan. No Project Manager, regardless of their level of experience, will possess all the knowledge necessary to create an accurate Project Plan. Including the right people, asking the right questions and creating easy-to-use documentation should be the focus of the Project Manager during the Planning stage.

Should there be a formal sign-off on the Project Plan from the Project Sponsor?

Whether or not a formal sign-off is needed on the Project Plan is an organizational decision. When determining if sign-off is needed, remember that the Project Plan is a detailed and sometimes technical document used by the project team to document the project approach. It may not be written in business terms. To hand a detailed plan over to the Project Sponsor and expect that they will read and internalize the entire document can be an unrealistic expectation.

What should occur is a review of the highlights of the Project Plan with enough detail for the Sponsor to make an informed decision to proceed, postpone or cancel the project.

If a project gets canceled at the end of Planning, isn't it the result of poor planning?

It could be the result of a poor plan, but it is more likely the result of a good business decision. Canceling a project before execution begins can be good when:

- Resources are not available to staff the project as planned.
- High-priority projects exist that will compete for resources and delay the project.
- The Business Case no longer shows positive value.

Execution (Execute the Plan)

Some project management methodologies split this stage into two stages that run in parallel:

- Execution stage – where the Project Plan is implemented
- Monitoring and Control stage – where project tracking and status reporting are completed

Separate or combined, the amount of work completed in the stages remains unchanged. For the purposes of this book, we will use the stage name Execution to include all the activities in Execution, Monitoring and Controlling.

Execution Key Components

Purpose: Implement the Project Plan by creating the project deliverables in order to achieve the project goals and satisfy the business need

Input: Project Plan and Business Case (optional)

Output: Updated Project Plan and an updated Business Case (optional), plus the decision to cancel or continue the project. Additional project management deliverables include Project Status Reports, Issue Log and Scope Change Log

The Planning stage overlaps with the Execution stage. During this overlap of stages, the Project Plan is updated as more detailed planning occurs and approved changes are made to the project. Any detail or approved changes that impact the overall financial justification in the Business Case requires an updated Business Case.

Additional project management deliverables include:

Project Status Reports – the status reports should be targeted to the unique information needs of the Sponsor. The Status Report's purpose is to help the Sponsor and Stakeholders understand the current status of the project. Common status reports may contain the following information:

- Reporting time frame
- Project description (or goal statement) – so that anyone who reads the status reports shares a common understanding of the project focus and purpose
- Status items – from two perspectives: where the project is today compared to the Project Plan, and a projection of

where the project should be at the end of the project based on current knowledge. Status should be reported on the following items: Stakeholders' KPI, issues, risks, financial and milestone progress

Issue Log – this log is used to track events that occur and require action during project execution. The Issue Log ensures that issues get the appropriate attention (don't get forgotten and slip through the cracks) and provides a historical reference for similar projects in the future. The Issue Log should  be accessible to everyone on the project team, and may contain the following information:

- Date the issue was first identified and documented
- Description of the issue
- Recommended action needed to manage or resolve the issues
- Name of the individual who identified, investigated or resolved the issue
- Status of the issue: open, under investigation or resolved/ closed

Change Log – this log is used to track requested changes (often referred to as scope change) to the project once the Project Plan has been approved in the Planning stage. The Change Log should be accessible to all on the project team, and may contain the following information:

- Date that the scope change request was first identified and was documented
- Description of the requested scope change

- Impact of *accepting the change* on the project work, staffing, timing, budget and value delivered if the requested change is approved
- Impact of *rejecting the change* on the project work, staffing, timing, budget and value delivered if requested change is rejected
- Alternative options that identify trade-offs that can be made to include the change (and remove something else from the project) that will not impact the timing or budget of the project
- Name of the individual who requested the scope change
- Status of the scope change: under investigation, approved or rejected

Execution Roles and Responsibilities

Icon	Project Role	Execution Responsibility
	Sponsor	Provides ongoing support for project work, communicates continued importance of the project, and communicates organization changes that could impact the project
	Stakeholders	Provide ongoing support for project work and share any changing business needs from their unique perspective
	Project Manager	Works with Sponsor and Stakeholders to keep them updated on project progress, provides leadership to project team, and keeps project documentation up to date

Icon	Project Role	Execution Responsibility
	Project Team	Completes project work, and provides continued expertise based on past projects and organizational experience

The Approach to Execution

The Execution stage of the project consumes the most resources in terms of time, staffing and funding. It is important during this stage that the Project Plan is followed in order to leverage the benefits of the team's collaborative planning efforts.

The Execution stage should begin with on-boarding the project team members through individual meetings or holding a team kick-off meeting. The remainder of the Execution stage should be spent completing the work defined in the Project Plan, on-boarding of new team members, managing issues, managing change requests, monitoring project progress, executing the communication plan, engaging Stakeholders, reevaluating risks and completing ongoing project planning.

Common Errors to Avoid

All too often, Project Plans are developed and then filed away. The execution of the project then follows a "seat of the pants" approach, not gaining any benefit from the planning work created by the project team.

Key Questions Answered in the Execution Stage

 During the Execution stage, project management tools and techniques continue to be applied to track project progress and provide the Project Manager with data that will assist in determining action items. The Project Manager will continue to ask and answer the following questions:

Questions	What the Answer will Provide
Is the work being done according to plan?	• Variances between planned and actual time and budget • Progress towards the Stakeholders' KPI
Are project changes being managed effectively? Are issues being resolved?	• The effectiveness of project management processes used to manage issues and scope changes
Are team members working well together?	• The status of the team dynamics, and whether or not there is a need for team building • The effectiveness of project leadership
Are project communications effective?	• Verification on whether or not individuals are getting the right project information when they need it

Common Questions About Execution

Why can't we just start here (at Execution); do we really need a plan?

Many projects start at Execution without much or any planning. These projects are similar to taking a vacation without an itinerary. If your vacation goal is to get away and relax, then it might not matter where you go, when you get there, what you take with you or how much you spend—and your vacation will be a success. If on the other hand, there are specific locations you would like to see, specific activities you would like to enjoy, limited funding and limited timing, then a plan will increase your probability of a successful vacation.

What does a vacation analogy have to do with project management? If you start your project without a Project Plan, then you don't really know where you are going, or how you will get there. It is very difficult to rally a team to work together without a clearly defined project strategy, or to have a clear understanding of when the project is complete. If these events are okay with you—and your organization—then begin without a Project Plan. On the other hand, if what you deliver, when you deliver and how you use resources are important, then Planning is critical to your project's success.

Should I follow the Project Plan? What if I get a better idea?

Project Plans are developed with the intention to be followed. As long as they continue to make sense, they should be followed. If they no longer make sense, or if you discover a better approach, then the Project Plan should be reevaluated, and you might want to revisit the Planning stage. When looking at changing the project approach during Execution, take into consideration the following items:

- What is the impact of changing the project approach on the project work, staffing, timing, budget and the value delivered?
- What is the impact of *not* changing the project approach on the project work, staffing, timing, budget and the value delivered?

Make sure that the new approach is presented to the Project Sponsor to gain his/her approval to the change.

I want to follow the Project Plan, but leadership keeps asking for more things, and different things. Now what?

Part of leading a successful project is managing the expectations of others. If others have a different vision of what your project should be doing, or delivering, then conversations like the one in this question will continue to occur. The best way to handle requests for changes to your project is to first clearly communicate the scope of the project. It is critical that everyone has a common understanding of the project scope. If scope is understood, and changes are still being requested, follow the project's change management process (Chapter 14). This process ensures that the right individuals are making informed decisions when modifying the approved scope of the project.

In organizations where there are no real costs associated with changing the project scope (meaning that it does not cost more money, or take the project longer—because the project team begins working unreported overtime), it is common for leadership to add to the project scope—without understanding the impact on the Project Plan or project team. Once the impact of the additional scope is communicated and leadership is asked to pay for the change, or delay project completion, then better business decisions will be made.

Managing scope this way is *not* meant to ignore the requests of leadership or the customer; it *is* meant to help them make informed decisions on how the changes to the project will impact project completion.

What happens if the Project Plan is wrong?

Maybe the work is not producing the value you expected, or things are taking longer than planned, or there are more risks than originally thought, or the team member skill sets do not meet the skills required in the Plan—the potential reasons for a Project Plan being wrong are many. Remember that a Project Plan is your best guess at the time the Project Plan is created. It should not be a surprise if the Project Plan needs to be updated, modified or corrected. Revisiting the Planning stage is a normal part of the project lifecycle. You must plan time in Execution for ongoing Planning.

Closing (Knowledge Capture and Learning)

Closing Key Components

Purpose: To formally close out the project and gather organizational learning that can be applied to other work

Input: Project Documentation, including the final Project Plan, Status Reports, Issue Log, Change Log and final Business Case (optional)

Output: Final Project Documentation, Lessons Learned and a Project Evaluation

The Closing stage should begin anytime a project is completed or canceled. The Closing stage is a brief time to gather the collective learnings of the project team and provide closure to the project. Common project management deliverables from Closing include:

Final Project Documentation – ensure that all project documentation is completed. This could include

archiving the Project Plan and related project documentation for future reference, ensuring that all required issues are closed, that all approved scope changes were delivered and closing out project charge codes.

Lessons Learned – document the knowledge that was acquired

during the project from the perspectives of the Stakeholders, Sponsor, Project Manager and project team members. This knowledge capture can be related to how project management was applied to the project, how the teams worked together and communicated to each other, as well as technical knowledge gathered from creating the project deliverables. It is important that this knowledge be shared with the project team and others in the organization that can leverage your project learnings for their project benefit.

Project Evaluation – this document provides an overall sum-

mary of the project and is a good go-to document for someone who wants to understand the project without investing a lot of time and digging into all the details of the project management documents. The Project Evaluation assesses the project's actual performance versus the planned performance, and highlights key improvements that can be leveraged for future projects. Common components of a Project Evaluation document include:

- Project overview – brief summary of the project goals and scope
- Findings – comparison of the project actuals to the original Project Charter, final Project Plan and industry standards (if they exist)
- Lessons Learned – brief summary of the key lessons learned from planning and executing the project
- Follow Up/Next Steps – recommendations for implementing key lessons learned into the organization and any follow-up action required at project completion

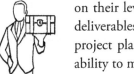

Stakeholder Satisfaction – gather feedback from Stakeholders on their level of satisfaction with the final project deliverables, communication provided during project planning and execution, and the project's ability to meet their KPI.

Team Member Feedback – constructive feedback on the individual contribution of each project team member. This should be completed by following any Human Resource guidelines that your organization may provide.

Closing Roles and Responsibilities

Icon	Project Role	Closing Responsibility
	Sponsor	Provides feedback on the project process and final value delivered by the project, provides resources necessary for Closing stage, and is willing to integrate organizational changes based on Closing stage learnings

Icon	Project Role	Closing Responsibility
	Stakeholders	Provide feedback on the project process and final value delivered by the project
	Project Manager	Facilitates Closing process and is willing to integrate changes to project management processes based on Closing stage learnings
	Project Team	Provides feedback on project process, and is willing to make changes to their processes and responsibilities based on Closing stage learnings

The Approach to Closing

The Closing stage of the project should occur anytime the project stops—at project completion or project cancelation. The purpose of the formal close is both administrative and reflective. The administrative work consists of closing out charge codes, paying all invoices and archiving project documentation for future access. The reflective portion of Closing should happen more than once in a large project. Reflection on lessons learned should occur at major milestones during the life of the project. Reflection can include:

- Survey to gather feedback on individual project contributor's perspective of the project work
- Interview of Stakeholders and team members to gather candid observations of project planning and execution

- Benchmarking against similar projects within the organization or within your industry
- Gathering project metrics to verify value delivered

Workshop Idea: Holding a Project Closing Workshop

A great way to formally close out a project, and celebrate project success and team contribution, is to hold a Closing Workshop. Before holding a Closing Workshop, interview Stakeholders and key team members to gather their individual feedback on the execution and outcome of the project. Gather project actuals and compare them to the original plan. Use this information to draft an initial Lessons Learned and Project Evaluation. Use the workshop to complete the closing documents by having the participants collaboratively answer the following questions:

- Are there any outstanding items that need to be addressed?
- What feedback have you heard about the project results?
- What did you learn on this project that can aid in the success of future projects? Focus both on what went well and what did not go well.
- How should the learning be shared with others? Focus on what should be shared with Sponsors, Project Managers and other teams.

Answering these questions will provide most of the information necessary to update the Closing documents.

Key Questions Answered in the Closing Stage

 During the Closing stage, the Project Manager will work with the entire project team to ask a final set of questions:

Questions	What the Answer will Provide
Was the work completed according to plan? • On time? • Within budget? • Meeting Stakeholders' needs? • According to industry best practices?	• Project Evaluation documentation
What would you do differently or the same if you were working on this project again?	• Lessons Learned

Common Questions About Closing

Do I really need to include the Closing stage; the project is over and I'd like to put it behind me?

Project Closing is where reflective learning occurs. How many times have you made the same mistake more than once? I

One of my clients said they skipped the Closing because, "Work was moving so fast that it was like being on a train driving 100 miles an hour while the track was still being laid." They were smart enough to know that this approach is a poor long-term strategy. Time for reflection, learning and planning is necessary to build sustainable success.

know I have—and it is often when I think I have too much to do to stop and be reflective—but a moment of reflection can save you rework and frustration.

Why does everyone need to be involved in Closing; isn't it just a Project Manager thing?

Although the project management deliverables are primarily the responsibility of the Project Manager, the Project Manager has only one perspective. This limited perspective will negatively impact the overall quality of the Lessons Learned and Project Evaluation.

Each department involved in the project should have a voice in reflective feedback on the project process in order to gain a clear understanding of the project's strengths and weaknesses.

Why bother documenting Lessons Learned; they just get filed away and ignored?

Lessons and learning are meant to be shared. Spend less time worrying about documentation (and less energy creating formal documentation) and more time creating a forum for sharing the learning that other projects will benefit from in the future.

Would it be better to have someone other than the Project Manager facilitate the Closing; people might not give candid answers?

If the Closing process involves face-to-face interviews or surveys with names on them, it is best to have someone other than the Project Manager facilitate the Closing process. Even the best Project Manager can create bias when asking reflective questions related to the project they just led.

If you want candid answers, an unbiased third party can best facilitate the Closing process.

I completed the Closing stage, as recommended, and nothing happened; now what?

> The value of the Closing stage is learning; and the value of learning is future improvements. Although the organization might not be willing to make changes based on the results of your project, it is still possible for you to learn and apply those learnings to your next project. So, don't be discouraged, continue your personal growth as a Project Manager.

Why use the Project Charter as a comparison document in Closing when I already know that the project final actuals will not be the same as the high-level estimates provided in the Initiation stage?

> Comparing project actuals to the final approved Project Plan creates the impression that the project was well planned and well executed. If you want to *learn* from the project, you must compare the Project Charter from the Initiation stage to the final project actuals. In this comparison, there will be a gap between the plan and actuals, and a larger opportunity to learn. You can ask questions like:
>
> * What have we learned through this project that will make estimating time, cost, resources and final output more accurate in the future?
> * Who should be involved in early estimating to increase the estimating accuracy for this type of project?
> * What have we learned from this project that will improve the engagement of Stakeholders in the future?
> * How can we share this learning with the organization?

Why should I provide team member feedback; none of the team reports to me?

> Even if you have no official requirement to provide feedback to members of your team, it is a value-added effort. Feedback creates

a win-win-win. A win for the team member—everyone likes specific recognition for their contribution; a win for the team member's direct manager—who may not be aware of the specific contributions of their resources; and a win for the Project Manager—when you provide valuable feed-

In post-project interviews at a client site, I asked a team member how the team knew when the project was over and if the product they created was successful. The team member's response was that they read industry periodicals to see if the products they worked on were launched. The lack of feedback creates low levels of engagement and can impact the dedication to future projects.

back to the team and management, people will be more motivated to work with you on future projects.

Chapter Summary

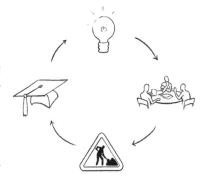

This chapter detailed the project management lifecycle phases or stages. The stages are interdependent and not necessarily linear.

All projects begin with an idea and enter the Initiation stage, where questions are answered and documented in a Project Charter. These questions help to define the preliminary scope of the project. Once a decision has been made to proceed with a project, the detailed planning, in the Planning Stage, begins. If the decision is made to continue the project, the Execution stage begins.

During the Execution stage, project deliverables are created, and the Project Manager is busy leading the project effort, updating the Project Plan and communicating project status.

If at any time a decision is made to cancel the project, the Closing stage begins. The Closing stage is also initiated after all project deliverables are created and accepted by the customer or Project Sponsor. The Closing stage evaluates the project and gathers lessons learned for the organization to improve future projects.

Section 2:

PROJECT MANAGEMENT TECHNIQUES

Techniques are presented to aid you in your project management application. The purpose of any technique is to speed up your ability to get work done in a standardized, repeatable and complete manner. Not all techniques are necessary on every project; and like anything, the more you understand it, and the more practice you have, the quicker it will help you get your job done.

When reviewing each technique, challenge yourself to understand the purpose of the technique and when to apply it on your project. Obviously, you can apply necessary techniques in the Planning stage and then continue ongoing planning during Execution; but know that it is not too late in Execution to apply any of these techniques for the first time.

Each chapter in this section will cover a project management concept that includes a review of one or more techniques with examples and illustrations, plus ideas for applying the technique in a collaborative workshop.

Chapter 3: Goals

> *"If you don't know where you are going,
> you will wind up somewhere else."*
> ~Yogi Berra, former catcher and manager for the
> New York Yankees

Projects should have clearly defined goals that are tied to the strategies, mission and vision of the organization, and support department priorities.

Having clearly defined goals answer the following questions:

- What will the project achieve?
- What does success look like?
- How will we know when we are done?

How many times have you been on a project team and not known the purpose of the project? For many, the answer is, "More often than I would like to admit."

Project goals set the focus for the project team. Goals should be clearly defined so that all team members and project stakeholders

If you don't know the project goal, it is hard to be an effective Project Manager or contributing team member.

have similar expectations of what the project will and will not achieve. We all have short attention spans, and many things vying for our attention, so we need an elevator speech—a way to share the goal in a clear and concise way.

If asked for the goal of your project, could you tell me in a sentence or two?

What if I asked project team members, would they all tell me the same goal?

In this chapter, the SMART technique for establishing goals will be reviewed.

Technique: Creating SMART Goals

A common acronym used to establish a project goal is SMART. If you search the Internet, you will find various definitions of the SMART acronym. Use the definition that is best fit for your organization. I use the definition described here, as it is a good fit for establishing clearly defined project goals.

S Specific – defines a common and clear project focus. Because we all bring different ideas and perspectives to the project, having a specific goal removes ambiguity. For example:

Ambiguous – Train

Better – Provide project management training

Best – Provide project management training to the sales staff

Measurable – defines how project success will be measured. The measure of success can be quantitative or qualitative. It should align with the project success criteria of your Stakeholders (see Chapter 4: Stakeholders). Examples of metrics include:

Ambiguous – Provide project management training to the sales staff

Better – Provide project management training to the entire sales staff

Best – Provide project management training to the entire sales staff, so that the sales team can execute their role as Project Sponsors

Action – The action portion of the goal statement is a verb that sets the overall project direction, but not the project approach. As illustrated in the table below, a goal statement should use the action verb only and not the approach. There are numerous potential approaches to achieve a project goal. The project approach may change, but the overall project direction is less likely to change.

Use the action verb in the SMART Goal statement: Sample Action Verbs	Do NOT use the Approach in the SMART Goal Statement: Sample Project Approaches
Train	Training approaches can include: classroom, on-the-job, coaching and mentoring, self-paced, web-based, job-aids, and more . . .
Research	Research can be completed through: focus groups, observation, surveys, experiments, pilots, tests and more . . .

The *project approach* should be determined by the project team collaboratively during the Planning stage; and the *action or direction* of the project should be established collaboratively between the Project Manager, Sponsor and Stakeholders.

 Realistic – determines if the SMART goal can be achieved. This is a simple but quick gut check, based on your past experience that tells you:

YES – the goal can be achieved

NO – the goal cannot be achieved as currently defined

UNSURE – more planning needs to be done to determine whether or not the goal is realistic

A word about stretch goals:

Do all goals need to be realistic? What about stretch goals? In some organizations, leaders like to

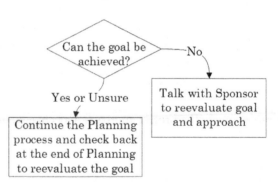

challenge their staff with stretch goals—ask for more than they think is possible, knowing that what is delivered will still stretch the team to deliver more than they thought was possible. These goals will rarely pass the realistic test. Remember that these techniques are guidelines to follow and adjust as necessary. They are not hard rules that mandate adherence, so stretch goals can be used.

 Time-bound – defines when the project goal will be achieved. A caution about time-bound: do not create arbitrary due dates. If legal, regulatory, contracts or other outside mandatory forces require a specific end date, then use that date. If there is not a hard date that the project needs to be done by, then pick a realistic time frame and add that date range to your goal statement.

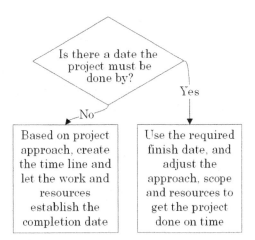

Using the SMART Goals Technique, our goal statement goes from:

Ambiguous – Train staff

Better – Provide project management training to the entire sales staff

Best – Provide project management training to the entire sales staff, so that the sales team can execute their role as Project Sponsors by end of first quarter 20xx.

Ensure that everyone who interacts with the project understands the SMART goal. Add the project goal statement to all project documentation and communications.

Workshop Idea: Establishing Common Project Goals

The planning workshop should begin with the Sponsor sharing the business need, project vision and project goal (although Sponsors rarely provide SMART goals).

At the end of the planning workshop, ask the team members to restate the project goal in their own words—work together to create a singular goal statement. After the team has spent time planning for the project, they may have a clearer, well-articulated and internalized SMART goal.

Goals Summary

Having clearly defined goals answer the following questions:

- What will the project achieve?
- What does success look like?
- How will we know when we are done?

Ensure that your project is aligned with the organization's vision, mission and strategies, and that the project supports your departmental objectives.

Create a SMART goal to ensure that the goal statement is: specific, measurable, action-bound, realistic and time-bound.

Add the project goal statement to all project documentation and communications so there is one common understanding of what the project will achieve.

> *"If you don't know where you are going,*
> *any road will get you there."*
> ~Lewis Carroll, author of *Alice's Adventures*
> *in Wonderland* and many other books

Chapter 4: Stakeholders

> *"Organizations can no longer choose if they want to engage with stakeholders or not; the only decision they need to take is when and how successfully to engage."*
> ~Neil Jeffery, Doughty Centre,
> Cranfield School of Management

Before we discuss the techniques for engaging Stakeholders, let's first answer some common questions.

What is a Stakeholder?

> A stakeholder is anyone who is actively involved in the project, or impacted by the execution or completion of the project. Stakeholders have expectations of what the project will deliver.

Who is a Stakeholder?

> A stakeholder can be anyone; for example a stakeholder can be a customer, client, vendor, partner, government, regulatory body, user, peer, team member or organizational leadership. The list of potential stakeholders can be quite long.

Why are Stakeholders important?

> Stakeholders have the ability to influence a project—they can be supportive or create obstacles that could delay or stop the project.

Each stakeholder is unique: some stakeholders will have a voice that can impact your project; other stakeholders may have no voice (they will have ideas and opinions, but, officially, they have no input into the project strategy). Because no two stakeholders are the same, we need to spend some time understanding the importance of stakeholders and how they should be managed within a project. In this chapter, we will review the different roles a stakeholder can play, and how to identify stakeholders, understand stakeholder relationships, assess stakeholder engagement, determine stakeholder perception and develop an action plan for engaging stakeholders in your project.

Technique: Providing Role Clarity

Not all stakeholders are equal. Stakeholders may play different roles within the organization, and within your project. Role clarity is necessary for developing a good working relationship with your stakeholders. In addition to being a stakeholder, an individual may fill one of the following additional roles:

Icon	Role	Project-Related Responsibilities
	Sponsor	• Is **or** represents the primary project benefactor • Accountable for project success • Sets the overall direction, and resolves critical business and project issues • Actively supports and empowers the Project Manager

Icon	Role	Project-Related Responsibilities
	Steering Committee	• Provides cross functional perspective • Works closely with the Sponsor • Provides overall support for project planning and execution • Holds formal ability to exert influence on the project
	Gatekeeper	• Makes project decisions for approval, re-scoping or rejection of project approach • Commits resources and funding to the project • Works closely with the Sponsor
	Project Manager	• Responsible for project success • Facilitates the application of project management to drive project success • Provides leadership to the project team
	Team Members	• Engage in collaborative project planning • Execute assigned work
	Subject Matter Experts	• Provide subject matter expertise on project strategy and project-related information

If an individual plays no other role on the project than Stakeholder, then they fill only the stakeholder's responsibilities of communicating their needs and holding an informal ability to exert influence on the project.

Technique: Identifying Stakeholders

Now that we know the different roles that stakeholders may play, let's look at the first step in actively managing the stakeholders on your project: identifying project stakeholders. Begin by brainstorming and asking key questions:

Who is impacted by the project work?

- Who is impacted by the project results?
- Who are the decision makers on the project strategy?
- Who holds the decision for providing resources and funding for the project?
- Who has knowledge that can help with the planning and execution of this project?

The Three Components of Stakeholder Identification:

1. Identify Stakeholders
2. Determine additional Stakeholder roles and overall Stakeholder priority
3. Understand Stakeholder relationships

When answering these questions, think both internal to the organization's functional areas and business processes as well as potential external stakeholders.

Not all stakeholders have equal priority on the project: part of stakeholder identification is to determine which additional roles might be played by each stakeholder as well as that stakeholder's priority.

High-priority stakeholders (referred to as Key Stakeholders) should be worked with closely to ensure that their business needs are satisfied. Medium- and lower-priority stakeholders need to be included in project communications and engaged

---

Key Stakeholders usually have:

• Higher interest in project execution and outcome
• Higher influence on project work
• Higher power and authority within the organization

---

enough to ensure that major issues are being addressed. Understanding each stakeholder's role will assist you in determining the priority of the stakeholder. Another way to differentiate between key and non-key stakeholders is that Key Stakeholders usually have more interest in the project execution or project outcome, more influence on the work being done, and more power and authority within the organization.

Understanding the relationships between stakeholders will be helpful later when building stakeholder management strategies. It may be helpful to know formal relationships, like who works for whom; and informal relationships, like which stakeholders are friends or respected colleagues.

This information can be documented in a stakeholder table, or graphically, using a stakeholder concept map. As an example, we will use the SMART goal—Provide project management training to the entire sales staff, so that the sales team can execute their role as Project Sponsors by end of first quarter 20xx. For this goal, if we asked, "Who is impacted by the project work and project results?" we might answer:

- The PMO who supports project management activities
- The trainers who will be providing project management training
- The sales staff who will receive project management training
- The project leads who run projects that the sales staff sponsor
- The sales managers who manage the sales staff

Documenting this information in a stakeholder table or concept map could look like this:

Stakeholder	Project Role	Relationships
Project Leads	Stakeholders	Report indirectly (dotted line) to PMO There is a lack of role clarity when they work with Sales
Training	Project Manager (for this project)	Collabortive working history with PMO Has worked with Project Leads in the past, but their relationship is unknown
Sales Staff	Stakeholder (and project client)	Reports to Sales Managers
Sales Managers	Stakeholders	Sales Staff reports to them
PMO	Sponsor	Indirectly manage (dotted line) Project Leads

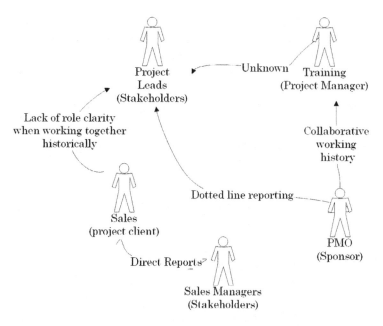

Figure 1: Stakeholder Concept Map

Workshop Idea: Stakeholder Identification and Prioritization

Completing stakeholder identification as a project team will aid you in developing a more complete list of stakeholders.

Provide small pads of sticky paper to the workshop participants. Have each participant identify all the potential stakeholders by answering these questions:

- Who is impacted by the project work?
- Who is impacted by the project results?
- Who are the decision makers on the project strategy?
- Who holds the decision for providing resources and funding for the project?
- Who has knowledge that can help with the planning and execution of this project?

Create a 2x2 matrix labeled "high power" and "low power" across the bottom (x axis), and "high interest" and "low interest" down the side of the matrix (y axis). Have each workshop participant place each stakeholder sticky in the appropriate cell in the 2x2 box based on what the stakeholder's power and interest should be for this project. For those stakeholders in the high-power and high-interest cell, create a stakeholder concept map or stakeholder table. These stakeholders are often referred to as Key Stakeholders.

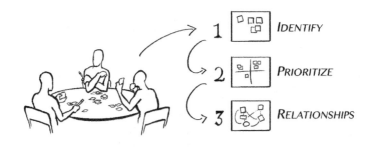

Technique: Assessing Stakeholder Engagement

Not only does each stakeholder have different roles and levels of priority on the project, each stakeholder may have a different level of engagement on the project.

There are many tools available to access and manage an individual's level of engagement. Most of these tools can be attributed to driving change in organizational behaviors. The specific source for the model we are reviewing is unknown. This model breaks engagement down into six levels:

Level of Engagement	Description
1. Unaware	No idea that the project exists
2. Aware	Aware of the project, but not aware of any project details
3. Understand	Aware of the project, and understands the project purpose, project strategy and key details of the project
4. Collaborate	Willing to work together with the project team as requested to support the project work
5. Commit	Willing to dedicate time and/or resources to project work
6. Advocate	Willing to proactively support the project through actions and communications

With these six levels of engagement in mind, reflect back on the Key Stakeholders, and assess for each:

- What is their current level of engagement with the project?
- What should their level of engagement be to drive project success?

If there is a Key Stakeholder that is unaware that the project exists, yet project success requires them to commit resources to the project, then there is a gap between their current level and desired level of engagement.

A stakeholder engagement assessment can be completed by simply updating your stakeholder concept map or stakeholder table to include their level of engagement.

Here is the updated table and map for the sample we have been using:

Stakeholder	Project Role	Relationships	Level of Engagement	
			Current	Desired
Project Leads	Stakeholders	Report indirectly (dotted line) to PMO There is a lack of role clarity when they work with Sales	Collaborate	Collaborate
Training	Project Manager (for this project)	Collabortive working history with PMO Has worked with Project Leads in the past, but their relationship is unknown	Commit	Commit
Sales Staff	Stakeholder (and project client)	Reports to Sales Managers	Unaware	Commit
Sales Managers	Stakeholders	Sales Staff reports to them	Aware	Advocate
PMO	Sponsor	Indirectly manage (dotted line) Project Leads	Advocate	Advocate

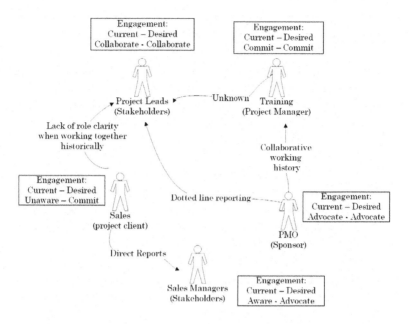

Figure 2: Updated Stakeholder Concept Map

Anytime there is a gap between the current level and desired level of stakeholder engagement, a strategy should to be developed to reduce or eliminate the gap. Because gaps in levels of engagement require additional work by the project team, make sure that you are focusing mainly on Key Stakeholders. There is limited value in moving a low-priority stakeholder from unaware to understand when there may be high-priority stakeholders that need to be moved from understand to commit.

Workshop Idea: Defining Stakeholder Engagement

After the Key Stakeholders have been identified, have the project team assess each stakeholder's current and desired state of engagement by creating a wall chart that lists each stakeholder down the side of the chart and level of engagement across the top. Split the participants into two groups:

- Have one group assess the current level of engagement, and place a colored mark or sticky in the appropriate cell.
- Have the other group assess the desired level of engagement for each stakeholder, and place a different colored mark or sticky in the appropriate cell.

End the activity with a discussion of the gaps between current and desired state.

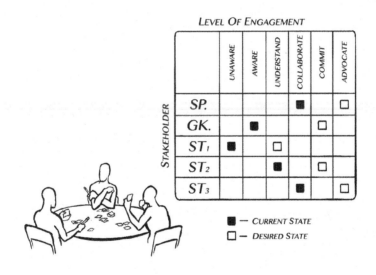

LEVEL OF ENGAGEMENT

STAKEHOLDER	UNAWARE	AWARE	UNDERSTAND	COLLABORATE	COMMIT	ADVOCATE
SP.				■		□
GK.		■			□	
ST₁	■		□			
ST₂			■		□	
ST₃				■		□

■ — CURRENT STATE
□ — DESIRED STATE

Technique: Determining Stakeholder Perceptions

Before you build a stake-
holder strategy, you will
need to understand the
perceptions of each stakeholder. Specifically, you

The following terms may be used
interchangeably: success criteria and
Key Performance Indicators (KPIs).

---

are attempting to look at the project from the stakeholders' view to
understand what they see. Stakeholder perceptions can be gathered
by asking a few questions, for example:

- What value does the stakeholder see, or want out of the
  project?
- What does success look like to them, and how will they
  measure it (success criteria are often referred to as Key
  Performance Indicators or KPIs)?
- What could they see that would cause them to resist or not
  support the project?

Value can be defined in many ways. For some stakeholders, value
can be measured from both business and personal perspectives. For
example:

> In *business* terms, value can be reduced cycle time, reduced
> cost, increased features or performance, customer satisfac-
> tion, quality metrics, sales targets, etc.

> In *personal* terms, value can be gaining new skills, exposure
> to leadership, opportunities for career growth, satisfying
> requirements on personal performance objectives, etc.

For each stakeholder, identify the criteria that they would use to
define project success. Ideally, Key Stakeholders will have similar or
supporting success criteria. Sometimes, Key Stakeholders can have
opposing or conflicting expectations of what project success looks

like. It is critical to hold conversations about expectations early in the project and engage the Project Sponsor in mediating any conflicting criteria that cannot be managed by the Project Manager.

Value is the positive perspective when reflecting on a project. The negative perspective or resistance to a project should be understood as well. Resistance can come in different ways. There may be resistance to change, or disagreement on project strategy and project success criteria. Resistance may be caused due to a gap in the stakeholder's level of engagement. When a stakeholder is unaware of the project, and the project requires them to be committed, then that gap in engagement can be perceived as resistance.

When identifying stakeholder perception, it is better if there is more value than resistance.

At the end of Planning, the Project Manager and team should challenge the Project Plan to ensure that the project can meet each of the Key Stakeholders' success criteria.

This new information about Key Stakeholders can be added to your conceptual map or table.

Here is the updated table and map for the sample project we have been using:

Stake-holder	Project Role	Relationships	Level of Engagement		KPI
			Current	**Desired**	
Project Leads	Stakeholders	Report indirectly (dotted line) to PMO There is a lack of role clarity when they work with Sales	Collaborate	Collaborate	Consistant behavior from active supporting Sponsors
Training	Project Manager (for this project)	Collabortive working history with PMO Has worked with Project Leads in the past, but their relationship is unknown	Commit	Commit	Meeting project time, cost and performance requirements
Sales Staff	Stakeholder (and project client)	Reports to Sales Managers	Unaware	Commit	?
Sales Managers	Stakeholders	Sales Staff reports to them	Aware	Advocate	Minimum disturbance to Sales daily work
PMO	Sponsor	Indirectly manage (dotted line) Project Leads	Advocate	Advocate	Meeting project time, cost and performance requirements

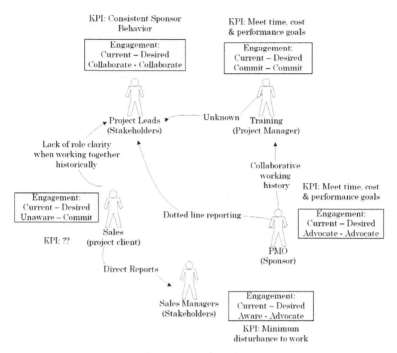

Figure 3: Final Stakeholder's Concept Map

Workshop Idea

When applying this technique in a workshop, a recommendation is to combine this technique with the Developing Stakeholder Management Strategies – the next technique we will be covering.

Technique: Developing Stakeholder Management Strategies

The data gathered to understand Key Stakeholders is valuable information for the Project Manager. Appropriately engaged stakeholders can help drive project success, just as disengaged stakeholders can derail what is otherwise a good project strategy.

How you use the data gathered about stakeholders will impact project execution.

When building a Stakeholder Management Strategy, begin by reviewing the stakeholder metadata:

- Current level of engagement
- Desired level of engagement
- Value – need that will be satisfied by the project
- Resistance – reasons they might not support or participate in the project
- Relationship – how each stakeholder is connected

After reviewing the data, begin your analysis by asking:

- Does the project value delivered match the stakeholder's perception?
- Where does the level of engagement need to be increased?
- Are there relationship gaps?
- Are there instances of:
  - More resistance than value
  - No defined value
  - Individuals unaware of value

Use this analysis to build your Stakeholder Management Strategy. For example: When a client requested new software to optimize work processes, the impacted staff was aware of the change, but project success required that they be advocates for the new software. It was known that there would be the common resistance to change and the uncertainty that comes with new processes and new software. The proposed stakeholder strategy was to embed key staff onto the project team, making them a part of the requirements and software selection team. This strategy required more active engagement by the Project Manager, but lead to quicker acceptance because the impacted staff participated in selecting the solution.

Here is a potential Stakeholder Management Strategy for the sample project we have been using:

Stakeholder	KPI	Strategy to Maximize Engagement
Project Leads	Consistant behavior from active supporting Sponsors	Have Project Leads attend training to understand Sponsor behavior expectations Interview Project Leads prior to training development to understand their needs
Training	Meeting project time, cost and performance requirements	Already fully engaged
Sales Staff	?	Interview selected Sales Staff to understand their needs and KPIs Utilize Sales Managers to drive up Sales Staff's engagement

Stakeholder	KPI	Strategy to Maximize Engagement
Sales Managers	Minimum disturbance to Sales daily work	Work with Sales Managers to design a training approach that they will support
PMO	Meeting project time, cost and performance requirements	Provide status and follow PMO project guidelines

These strategies should be integrated into the project scope.

Stakeholder management is not a one-time event; revisit the strategies to update relationships, values, resistance and level of engagement.

Ideally, the final map:

- Is void of resistance
- Has stronger relationships
- Has matching current and desired engagement levels

Workshop Idea: Developing a Stakeholder Management Strategy

To focus on a complete Stakeholder Management Strategy in a team planning (or workshop) setting:

1. Complete the stakeholder identification workshop activity and level of engagement activity. Have the result of these two activities visible for the workshop participants to see.
2. Divide the team into groups. (The number of groups will be dependent on the number of participants in the workshop.) Split the number of Key Stakeholders amongst each group, so that each group is focusing on only a few Key Stakeholders.
3. For each Key Stakeholder, have each group review the previously defined information for the stakeholder, and create a flip chart for each stakeholder that documents the answers to the following:
    a. What value do they see or want out of the project?
    b. What does success look like to them, and how will they measure it (success criteria or KPIs)?
    c. What could they see that would cause them to resist or not support the project?
4. Based on this information, each group should discuss:
    a. Does the planned project value match the stakeholder's perception?
    b. Where does the level of engagement need to be increased?
    c. Are there relationship gaps?
    d. Are there instances of:
        i.   More resistance than value?
        ii. No defined value?
        iii. Individuals unaware of value?
5. Based on this discussion, the group should create specific recommendations to address any identified gaps and document them on the flip chart.
6. Each group should share their findings with the entire team, and then discuss and refine an agreed to Stakeholder Management Strategy.

The Project Manager is responsible for validating the outcome of the stakeholder assessments and integrating the strategies into the Project Plan.

STAKEHOLDER	KPI	STRATEGY

Stakeholders Summary

There are four steps to actively managing stakeholders. Determine which steps will bring the most value to your project, and focus on them as you develop your Stakeholder Management Strategies.

Step/Description	Questions to Ask/Answer
1. Stakeholder identification and relationship mapping	• What value do they see, or want out of the project? • How are people connected?
2. Assess level of stakeholder engagement	• What is their current level of engagement with the project? • What should their level of engagement be?

Step/Description	Questions to Ask/Answer
3. Determine stakeholder perception	• What value do they see, or want out of the project? • What does success look like to them, and how will they measure it (success criteria or Key Performance Indicators)? • What could they see that would cause them to resist or not support the project?

4. Analyze and develop the Stakeholder Management Strategy	• Does the project value delivered match the stakeholder's perception?
	• Where does the level of engagement need to be increased?
	• Are there relationship gaps?
	• Are there instances of:
	   ○ More resistance than value?
	   ○ No defined value?
	   ○ Individuals unaware of value?

"All stakeholders are equal, but some stakeholders are more equal than others"
-George Orwell, Eric Arthur Blair
journalist and author of *Animal Farm*

Chapter 5: Knowledge

> *"There are no secrets to success. It is the result of preparation, hard work, and learning from failure."*
> ~Colin Powell, American statesman and a retired four-star general in the United States Army

Sometimes, in our project planning, we are moving forward so quickly that we do not make the time to look back and reflect on what we already know. In project management, knowledge is all about leveraging the lessons learned on other projects, and applying them to current and future work.

We are limited by our own knowledge. No matter how much experience we have, it is all we know, and it limits us individually. This limit can afflict us with the thought that because of our experience and ability, we know better than individuals with less experience and ability. In some cases, this may be true; however, in most cases, there is much to be learned from others and their experiences.

The discipline of managing knowledge in a project is to share and harvest the experiences of the entire team so that, collectively, the experiences brought to project planning is far better than any one individual can produce.

In this chapter, we will discuss techniques for leveraging past learning and capturing learning for future work.

Technique: Leveraging Past Learning

The purpose of leveraging past learning is to gather what is already known that will help drive project success. There are two approaches for leveraging past learning—individual conversations and team brainstorming—and both can provide great value to planning. I am a proponent of applying both techniques as part of the planning process.

Approach: Individual Conversations

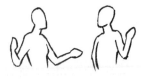

Let's start by talking about individual conversations, as not everyone is on the project team, and not everyone will be available to participate in a team planning process. Pick key people to meet with: individuals who managed similar type projects, or projects with similar resources or customers. Schedule some one-on-one time to briefly talk about your project and set the tone for why you want to gather their knowledge. Make sure during the individual conversations that you are spending more time listening than speaking. Your goal is to understand their experience first and then, second, to challenge yourself to identify ways to apply their experience to your project. Once the tone is set, and you are ready to listen, begin with some open-ended divergent questions (allowing the conversation to move in many different directions), such as:

- What have you learned?
- What drove project success?
- What created barriers, and how were they handled?

- How did you keep the Sponsor and Key Stakeholders engaged?
- How did you keep the team motivated?
- How did you keep everyone informed?

If there is time left in your meeting, wrap up by asking some convergent questions (convergent conversations bring you from many different directions back to the main area of focus—in this case, your project) that will focus on your project, such as:

- How would you recommend your experience gets applied to current projects?
- What is the one thing we should absolutely do? Not do?

Make sure you thank them for their time and their investment in the success of your project.

Approach: Team Brainstorming

Team brainstorming leverages past learning from the project team in a group environment. This shared learning also celebrates what the team has done well, so that it can be repeated, and identifies what has not gone well, so that it can be avoided. Start by setting the ground work of why you are leveraging past learnings—so we can repeat the good activities and avoid bad activities; and that the team is the best source of past learnings.

When working in a group, it is important that all voices are heard and that differences of opinions are welcome. The point of the discussion is not to come up with answers (yet) but to start by sharing experiences. The team conversation, like the individual conversations, should start divergent and then move to convergent.

Begin by having the team share positive experiences on projects that they felt were successful. They can wrap up their conversations by identifying the top characteristic of positive events on past projects.

Next, move to sharing the things they did not like, and have them wrap up their conversations by identifying the top things that should *not* be part of this project. Share the top ideas with the entire team.

This list of positives and "not to do's" should be audited into the Project Plan. For example, if the team states that:

- Having team building events were good ideas, then, in the project schedule, there should be team building events.
- Walk-throughs of drafted deliverables with Key Stakeholders were good ideas, then walk-throughs should be included in the project schedule.
- Withholding information (for example, only having access to project information at team meetings) slowed down past projects, then work to ensure that this will not happen again (for example, create a project site that has real-time information available to and accessible by the project team).

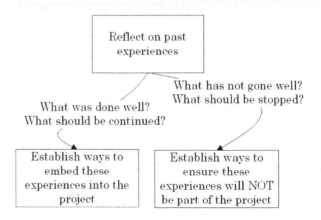

Whether through individual conversations or team planning, make sharing past project experience a part of your planning process. Ensure that you are doing more than talking; you need to listen, change the project approach to include positive learning and avoid negative practices.

Workshop Idea: Gathering Best Practices for the Project

Completing this activity as a project team will help reinforce to the team that their input is important and their past experience is valued.

Provide small pads of sticky paper to the workshop participants. Have each participant reflect on past projects and document on the sticky notes: *what has gone well on previous projects* and *what they would like to avoid on this project.* Label two flip charts (or whiteboards): *Best Practices to Embed* and *Events to Avoid.* Have the participants post their sticky notes on the appropriate chart.

As the project plan is developed, look for specific activities to add to the project to embed best practices and avoid the negative experiences.

Leveraging past learning helps improve current projects. Now, let's talk about techniques for capturing current learning to improve future projects.

Technique: Capturing Current Learning

Anytime the project ends—at project Closing or if the project is canceled; and for large initiatives, at major stage completion—lessons learned should be captured. These lessons learned can be shared with the organization to improve future projects.

We will look at capturing lessons learned as a process that includes: identifying participants to participate in sharing lessons learned, determining the baselines that will be used to evaluate the project actuals against, analyzing the feedback, and finally documenting and presenting the lessons learned.

```
┌──────────────┐  ┌──────────────┐
│  Identify    │  │   Gather     │
│  diverse     │  │  originally  │
│ participants │  │  promised    │
│  to gather   │  │  baselines   │
│  learnings   │  │              │
└──────────────┘  └──────────────┘
         │
         ▼
┌──────────────────┐
│     Gather       │
│  feedback on     │
│    project       │
│  actuals and     │
│  participants'   │
│   experiences    │
└──────────────────┘
         │
         ▼
┌──────────────────┐
│    Analyze       │
│    feedback      │
└──────────────────┘
         │
         ▼
┌──────────────────┐
│    Document      │
│  and present     │
│    lessons       │
│    learned       │
└──────────────────┘
```

Begin by identifying participants that should take part in sharing lessons learned. Participants of the project review should be as diverse as the participants in the project. Make sure that core and support team members from different organizational areas participate. Each organizational area will have different experiences. Consider including: core team members, Sponsor, Key Stakeholders and customers.

Early in the process, determine the baselines that will be used to evaluate the project actuals. Baselines are the agreed on project scope originally documented in the Project Charter and then updated in the Project Plan. Baselines can include the planned business value, project goal, final deliverables, timing, budget, resources and industry standards. Industry standards are standard metrics used to evaluate your project against, for example:

- Price per foot on new construction
- Number of hours necessary to create an hour of classroom training
- Cost per pound
- Cost per foot

Next, gather feedback from two sources:

- **The project team** – Team assess-ments help a project team improve the way they work together, increasing individual and team productivity. Questions should  focus on the effectiveness of communications, meetings, team dynamics, role clarity and collaborative planning. This data can be gathered in facilitated sessions or through online anon-ymous surveys.

- **Project actuals** – Actuals provide data on what really occurred on the project. Actuals can be: business value delivered, goals achieved, deliverables created, actual timing, actual budget and resources used.

Once the data and the baselines are gathered, analyzing can begin. Analyze the feedback captured, and then compare that data to the project baselines and industry standards to identify what went well and what could have gone better. These findings become the project's Lessons Learned and can be developed into best practices.

Workshop Idea: Capturing Lessons Learned for Future Projects

Completing this activity as a project team at major deliverable completion or project completion offers a great opportunity to recognize the work completed and provide motivation for future projects.

When gathering reflection on a specific project, it is good practice to break the team up into groups with similar project roles. Otherwise, if there is a builder and a tester at the same discussion table, they might not provide candid feedback. Use a selection of these questions to prompt the table decisions:

- What have you learned?
- What drove project success?
- What created barriers, and how were they handled?
- How did the team stay motivated?
- How effective were project communications?
- How would you recommend your experience gets applied to other projects?

Have each group share the highlights of their table discussions with the entire team; focusing on key knowledge captured and recommendations for other projects.

Use this information, along with the project baselines and actuals data, to create a Project Evaluation.

The last step in capturing lessons learned is documenting and presenting findings. The lessons learned will become input into the Project Evaluation document that is created in the Closing stage. Make sure to share your findings with the project team, Sponsor, PMO (if there is one) and other Project Managers that will benefit from understanding the experiences of your project.

Knowledge Summary

Leveraging past learning and capturing learning for future work ensures that we minimize past mistakes and benefit from past experience. When thinking about knowledge, remember to:

Reflect on past projects through individual conversations and during collaborative team planning by asking questions, such as:

- What have you learned?
- What drove project success?
- What created barriers, and how were they handled?
- How did you keep the Sponsor and Key Stakeholders engaged?
- How did you keep team members motivated?
- How did you keep everyone informed?
- How would you recommend your experience gets applied to current projects?
- What is the one thing we should absolutely do? Not do?

Capture lessons learned for use in future projects by following a process that includes:

1. Identifying individuals that should participate in sharing lessons learned.
2. Determining the baselines.

3. Gathering feedback from the project team and project actuals.
4. Analyzing the feedback captured, and comparing that data to the project baselines and industry standards.
5. Documenting and presenting findings to the project team and others that would benefit from the findings.

> *"Real knowledge is to know the extent of one's ignorance."*
> ~Confucius, Chinese teacher, editor, politician and philosopher

Chapter 6:
Deliverables

The purpose of the project is to create a tangible result (which, in project management terminology, is called a deliverable). In this chapter, we will talk about the need to identify all the deliverables created in Planning, Execution and Closing. In some organizations, the

> Deliverables are a component of the project scope. It is critical to clearly define what will and will not be created as a result of the project so that there is a common understanding of the scope and the ability to manage scope changes in the future.

term deliverable might be called outcome, output or artifact. For our purposes, we will use the term deliverable. Once all the deliverables are identified, you can begin to identify the work, resources and the costs associated with creating the deliverables.

Projects can produce many deliverables. We can identify deliverables by answering three questions:

1. What needs to be turned over at the end of the project to meet the business need?

2. What needs to be developed before the end of the project to support the creation of the final deliverables and drive the change required by the project?

3. What needs to be created to manage the project, motivate the team and provide project communications?

In this chapter, we will review techniques for identifying deliverables and creating a Work Breakdown Structure (WBS), which is also referred to as a Decomposition Diagram.

Technique: Identifying Deliverables

Once the project goal is defined, identifying what your project will deliver is the heart of project scoping. There are three categories of deliverables on all projects: final, interim and project management. Here is a definition of each deliverable category along with a small sample of potential deliverables.

Final Deliverables

Final deliverables are those deliverables turned over at the end of the project to meet the business need. Final deliverables can include, but are not limited to:

Facilities, projects, policies, metrics, software, documentation, procedures, training, training curriculum, annual meetings, consumer products and services . . .

The list of potential project deliverables is as long as, or longer than, the list of potential projects. So, it is critical that you gain agreement with the Sponsor and Key Stakeholders on the final deliverables for your project.

Interim Deliverables

Interim deliverables are those deliverables that need to be developed before the end of the project to support the creation of the final deliverables. Interim deliverables can include, but are not limited to:

Designs, layouts, documentation, training strategies, implementation plans, test plans, organizational change management plans, maintenance plans, requirements, designs, drafts, pilots, prototypes, samples, benchmarking . . .

As you review the list, you may think some items listed here could be used as a final deliverable, and you are right. Depending on the project, what serves as an interim deliverable on one project, may be a final deliverable on another project.

It is also possible, on small projects, that there are no interim deliverables, only final and project management deliverables.

Project Management Deliverables

The most under-scoped category of deliverables includes those items that will be created to manage the project, motivate the team and provide project communications. Project management deliverables include:

Communications, meeting agendas and meeting minutes, budgets, contracts, status reports, project metrics, rewards and recognition, Project Plan updates, Project Evaluation and Lessons Learned.

Even when these deliverables are not included in the project planning, you will still be responsible for creating them; however, you will not have scheduled the time, resources and cost to create them.

Technique: Creating a Work Breakdown Structure (WBS)

The WBS (also known as a Decomposition Diagram) is a project management term used to reference breaking all the project work down in a hierarchical and structured or organized manner.

If you draw a WBS, it looks like an organization chart.

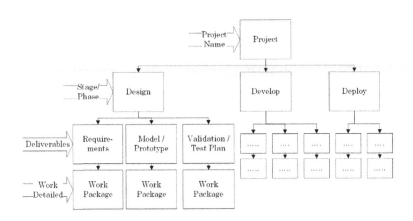

A WBS can be created in a diagram view or as a numbered list.

At the highest level of the diagram or indented list is the Project Name.

The next level of detail may represent how the project is organized if there are project phases. For example:

- Design, Develop and Deploy (as seen in the samples)
- Analyze, Design, Build, Implement
- Idea, Research, Develop, Test, Analyze, Implement

Project phases are not necessary; however, phases can be an effective way to organize a larger project to ensure that there is a common understanding of what work is being completed at a specific point

WBS Indented list:

0. Project
1. Design
  1.1 Requirements
    1.1.1 Work package elements
  1.2 Model/Prototype
    1.2.1 Work package elements
  1.3 Validation
    1.3.1 Work package elements
2. Develop
  2.1 ...
    2.1.1...
  2.2 ...
    2.2.1...
3. Deploy
  3.1 ...
    3.1.1...
  3.2 ...
    3.2.1...
  3.3 ...
    3.3.1...

in time (for example, during the Design phase, work should only be completed on Design phase deliverables and project management deliverables). At the next level of detail, deliverables are identified. Identify deliverables by answering the following questions:

1. What needs to be turned over at the end of this phase or stage?
2. What needs to be developed within the stage to support the creation of the final deliverables and drive the change required by the project?
3. What needs to be created to manage the project, motivate the team and provide project communications?

For each deliverable, the subsequent levels of the WBS document the work necessary to create the deliverable. This detail of work is referred to as a Work Package (see Chapter 8).

A sample WBS for the Sponsor's Sales training project might look like this:

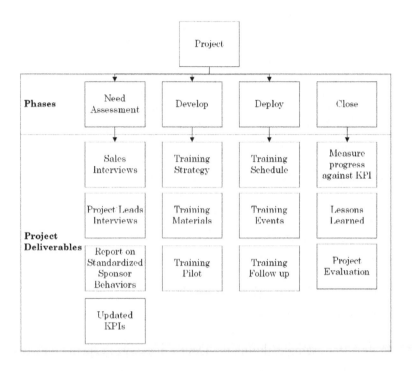

Workshop Idea: Defining Project Deliverables

Once the workshop participants understand the purpose of the project and what success looks like, have each participant identify all the deliverables (or major activities, if they are having a difficult time thinking of deliverables) that have to be created for the project to finish successfully. Use the deliverable-related questions to promote deliverable identification:

1.   What needs to be turned over at the end of the project to meet the business need?

2. What needs to be developed before the end of the project to support the creation of the final deliverables and drive the change required by the project?
3. What needs to be created to manage the project, motivate the team and provide project communications?

Each deliverable/major activity should be written on individual sticky notes. These sticky notes will be used later in the workshop to create the project schedule.

Deliverables Summary

Deliverable identification provides a tangible definition of what is in and what is out of project scope. There are three types of deliverables that should be identified on any project: final, interim and project management. Deliverables can be identified by asking the following questions:

1. What needs to be turned over at the end of the project to meet the business need?
2. What needs to be developed before the end of the project to support the creation of the final deliverables and drive the change required by the project?
3. What needs to be created to manage the project, motivate the team and provide project communications?

Once all the deliverables are identified, ask, "If these deliverables are created, will the project goal be achieved?" If the answer is yes, then the project scope is getting clearer; if the answer is no, or you don't know, then more work needs to be done in scoping the project.

"He who fails to plan, is planning to fail."
~Sir Winston Leonard Spencer-Churchill,
British politician and former Prime Minister
of the United Kingdom

Chapter 7: Quality

> *"Quality means doing it right when no one is looking."*
> ~Henry Ford, American industrialist and
> founder of the Ford Motor Company

Quality is about meeting customer needs, and ensuring that the project meets expectations. Quality answers the question: how will you ensure that the project deliverables will meet stakeholder expectations?

Quality focuses not only on the outcome of the project, but also on the process used to deliver the outcome. Traditionally, quality refers to:

- Quality Planning – establishing a plan to ensure that the project delivers to expectations
- Quality Control and Assurance – monitoring and auditing the project to ensure that the project is complying with company policies and procedures and the Quality Plan

In this chapter, we are going to focus on a tactical approach to identifying the expected level of quality through the use of defining and prioritizing quality requirements, and verifying quality while monitoring project progress.

Technique: Defining Quality Requirements

Requirements define the expectations of a project. Requirements are often defined in terms of features, functions or value delivered. Requirements can be defined at many levels. The most common approach to defining requirements would be to create a high-level requirements document in the Initiation stage—to provide some clarity on what is needed from the project. This is followed by more detailed requirements documentation in the Planning stage, which is finalized in the Execution stage. This approach to defining requirements focuses on the final deliverable. While it is important to define the quality and characteristics of the final deliverable, it can be short sighted to only focus on the end deliverable.

Two main strategies for defining project quality:

1. Defining only requirements for the final deliverable. This strategy is like the "big bang" or miracle approach, in that you do the work, and "bang," a miracle occurs, and the project delivers.

2. Designing interim requirements along the way—increasing the probably that the final deliverable will meet the requirements.

Let's simplify this by walking through an example. It is summer, and your mind keeps wandering off to the thought of ice cream. You know the kind: custard made with real dairy cream and real vanilla, served on a freshly made waffle cone (feel free to replace the example with your own favorite ice cream selection). When you place your order and receive your ice cream, you have expectations (we call these requirements) that the treat should satisfy in the form of size, texture and flavor. You know it when you see it. With that first taste, you will know if the ice cream meets your expectations.

In our ice cream example, our expectations (requirements) are for the final deliverable (ice cream) that we receive. For our requirements to be met, we make the assumption that all the steps taken to create the ice cream will support meeting the final requirements. For example: the procurement of raw ingredients are fresh, a  proven recipe is followed when creating your batch of ice cream, and the ice cream is stored in a frozen state and in sanitary conditions.

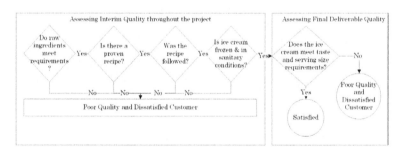

Assessing quality throughout the project provides an early warning that the final deliverable will or will not meet final expectations.

How do we apply this to your project? For each final, interim and project management deliverable, answer the following questions:

Who should establish the requirements?

The primary user of the deliverable should establish the requirements for the deliverable. In our ice cream example, it may be that the chef sets the requirements for the ingredients and the recipe, while someone from the Health Department may set the requirements for storage temperature and sanitary conditions, and a customer representative sets the requirements for serving size, final texture and flavor requirements.

It is important that the right person establishes deliverable requirements. If the Project Manager sets all requirements, they will be providing a best guess, and will likely miss something.

What are the requirements?

Once you have identified who should establish the requirements, it is time to list the requirements for each deliverable. Make sure that each requirement provides measurable or quantifiable expectations of what the deliverable will contain or be able to do. Requirements such as "better, faster, friendlier" provide more ambiguity than clarity. Ensure that the right individuals agree on the requirements and how they will be verified. In our ice cream example, for the storage facility, frozen is not a good requirement, but average temperature between 6°F and 10°F is a good and easy way to verify the requirement. Requirements can be documented in a table, for example:

Interim Deliverable	Requirements
Recipe	Must be tested and repeatable; include ingredients, measures and step-by-step instructions

Interim Deliverable	Requirements
Ingredients	Must be sourced within 100 miles, must be organic, must be received fresh weekly
Storage Facility	Average temperature between 6°F and 10°F, meets health codes for sanitary conditions, holds more than 50 gallons of ice cream, locks, lights up when open and is made of stainless steel
Serving of individual ice cream	Use standardized cone, use ice cream made within 3 days, ice cream serving is 6 oz.

How will requirements ensure that Key Stakeholder expectations are met?

Earlier, when discussing Key Stakeholders (Chapter 4), we introduced the concept of success criteria. Deliverable requirements should support the success criteria of Key Stakeholders and provide a tangible way to monitor the project's ability to meet success criteria during project execution.

Are requirements always needed?

If there are standards, guidelines or a template for a deliverable, then following those standards, guidelines or the template take the place of creating requirements. For example, if you need to secure capital funding for your project, then one of your project deliverables will be a Capital Funding request. If your organization has a standard template (or form) and procedure for a Capital Funding request, then defining requirements is not necessary. Requirements are necessary when you need to create a common understanding of what a deliverable is expected to do or how it is expected to perform.

Do I have to know all the requirements before the project starts?

> The answer is both yes and no: yes, if you have a small project, it is possible that you can identify most requirements in the Planning process; no, if the project is larger, or if one deliverable is dependent on a previous deliverable. For example, I can't know the requirements for something that is being built if it has not been designed yet. In this case, requirements may be defined right before you begin creation of each deliverable.

How do requirements tie back to SMART project goals?

> In order to achieve the project goal, the project must create deliverables. Each deliverable should have requirements to ensure that the interim deliverables are good enough so that the final deliverable meets the project's measure of success defined in the goal statement. If the interim deliverables are poor, it is likely that poor quality will accumulate into a final deliverable that will not meet expectations. We need to build toward requirements throughout the entire project, not just test for it at the end.

Technique: Prioritizing Requirements

Not all requirements are equal. The more requirements you have for any specific deliverable, the better you will understand what the deliverable should do, or how it should perform. Be careful when defining requirements that the list does not become a wish list of all the things you would *like* that deliverable to do, but does not actually need to do. Over-building requirements will increase the amount of work, resources and funding necessary to complete the project.

Once your list of requirements is complete, ask, which requirement:

Must be met in order for the deliverable to be usable?

Should be met?

Could be met?

Won't be met?

This prioritization technique is called MoSCoW. MoSCoW'ing your requirements ensures that the project work is meeting the *must* requirements, while only adding the work for should and could requirements if time, funding and resources allow.

If we apply MoSCoW to our ice-cream storage facility, our list might look something like this:

- Must – Average temperature between 6°F and 10°F
- Must – Hold 50 gallons of ice cream
- Should – Lock
- Should – Light up when open
- Could – Stainless steel
- Won't – Play music when opened

As long as the storage facility meets the "must" requirements, it will support the overall project goal.

Workshop Idea: Defining Deliverable Quality

Once project deliverables have been identified, the project team can define the requirements that should be met by deliverable to ensure that the project meets Stakeholder KPIs and the project goal.

Begin by identifying deliverables that do not have a standard definition—the ones that there can be ambiguity about what should or should not be included in the deliverable. For each of these deliverables, assign them to a workshop team that consists of customers (or users) of the deliverable, and have them answer the following questions:

1. Are there any templates, standard formats or work processes that we should be following when creating the deliverable?
2. Does the deliverable need to adhere to any external standards?
3. Who should establish the requirements for this deliverable?
4. What are the requirements that need to be met by this deliverable?

Once the questions are answered, prioritize the requirements, using the MoSCoW technique; and ensure that the requirements can be validated.

DEL.	REQUIREMENTS
A	M —— —— S —— —— C —— —— ——
B	M — C ——
C	M — - W — - - -

Technique: Monitoring Quality Progress

The purpose of monitoring deliverable quality is to assess the ability of the project deliverables to meet their defined requirements. Monitoring quality is essential. If your project is on time and on budget, but does not deliver to expectations, then the business need is not met; and the Sponsor, Key Stakeholders and the customers are not satisfied.

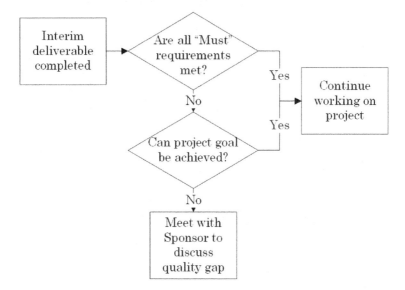

If requirements have been established for interim project deliverables, then monitoring quality along the way is simple. After each interim deliverable is created, audit that deliverable against the prioritized requirements. If all the "must have" requirements are met, then the project is meeting quality requirements. If any "must have" require- ments are missed, then determine how the final project quality will be impacted, and make adjustments to get the project back on track from a quality perspective. If requirements are missed, and cannot be met, putting the final project quality in jeopardy, then have a conversation with the Project Sponsor right away. If a project has a possibility of not delivering to the business need, it is best to have an early conversation to discuss the quality gap, and either modify the project approach or cancel the project. It is always better to cancel a project early than to continue working on a project that will not deliver to expectations.

Quality Summary

Quality is all about defining what project success and deliverable acceptance looks like from your customer's perspective. Determine which of your project's final and interim deliverables need clear requirements; for each deliverable, ask:

- Who should establish the requirement?
- What are the requirements?
- Are the requirements aligned with Key Stakeholder success criteria?
- What are the requirement priorities?

Once requirements are established, make sure to monitor the deliverable's ability to meet quality requirements throughout the project. Do not wait until project completion to ensure that project quality is met.

See Appendix D for an example of the deliverables and acceptance criteria for our sample project: Provide project management training to the entire sales staff, so that the sales team can execute their role as Project Sponsors by end of first quarter 20xx.

> *"The quality of your work, in the long run, is*
> *the deciding factor on how much your services*
> *are valued by the world."*
> ~Orison Swett Marden, American spiritual author

Chapter 8: Work

"The only place success comes before work is in the dictionary."
~Vince Lombardi, American football player, coach and executive

Getting the right work done ultimately drives project completion. When planning, make sure that the project team is doing the work, and only the work necessary to create each project management, interim and final deliverable at the level of quality defined in the deliverable requirements. If that work is completed and the deliverables are created, then the project goal will be achieved, the customer will be satisfied and the project will be considered a success.

In this chapter, we will focus on the application of the work package technique used to create estimates of effort, duration and resource requirements. The work package will help answer the following questions:

- What work needs to be done?
- How long will the work take?
- How many resources do we need to complete the work?
- How will we know when the work is completed?

Technique: Developing Work Packages

The WBS, introduced previously (Chapter 6: Deliverables), is used to organize and identify project deliverables. The lowest level of detail in the WBS is the work package.

The work package is ultimately the project "to-do list." The work package lists all the work that needs to be done to create each deliverable at the level of quality defined in the deliverable requirements.

The work package contains:

- Work Items – the "to-do list" of all work necessary to create the deliverable and meet the prioritized requirements (must haves)
- Effort – amount of time it will take for each work item to be completed
- Resource – the name, job title or department that will be responsible for completing the work
- Completion Criteria – metrics that tie back to the deliverable requirements to clarify when the work is completed (this is an optional component that can be added to help the team focus more on meeting requirements and less on just completing work items)

Terms:

Work Package – a bundle of work that, once completed, creates a completed deliverable or portion of a deliverable

Effort – how much time it takes to complete the work without the consideration of the calendar (e.g., 8 hours of effort)

Duration – total time to complete the work, taking into consideration the effort, calendar days plus the availability of resources (e.g., 8 hours of effort for a person who is working only 20 percent of the time on the project will take a duration of 5 days)

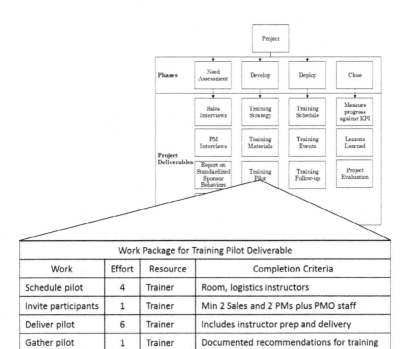

Work Package for Training Pilot Deliverable			
Work	Effort	Resource	Completion Criteria
Schedule pilot	4	Trainer	Room, logistics instructors
Invite participants	1	Trainer	Min 2 Sales and 2 PMs plus PMO staff
Deliver pilot	6	Trainer	Includes instructor prep and delivery
Gather pilot feedback	1	Trainer	Documented recommendations for training material updates

The work package provides critical information to the Project Manager. The work package is where the triangle for each deliverable comes to life. Information from the work package that defines the triangle includes:

- Time – effort estimates and resources allocation determine project duration
- Cost – effort estimates and resources, along with a fully loaded labor rate, will provide the information necessary to determine cost

- Scope – completion criteria (detailing what work is done to meet the deliverable quality requirements) determine scope

For each deliverable, there is now enough information to determine how long it will take to create, what resources are needed, how much it will cost and how you will verify that the deliverable is complete.

Here are some common questions and answers about creating work packages:

How granular should work be defined?

Identify work that can be completed between eight hours and forty hours. The low end (eight hours) ensures that you don't detail the work so much that it takes more time to create the list of work than it does to complete the work. The high end (forty hours) ensures that you don't identify the work in such large chunks that it does not provide enough guidance.

Does every deliverable need a work package?

The answer is no, if the work to create the deliverable is less than forty hours of effort or if the work has been operationalized (there is a standard, known way to create the deliverable); or if it is not important to know in advance what the work is, who the resources will be or how long it will take to create the deliverable.

The answer can be yes, if the deliverable will take more than forty hours of effort to create; or if you need an accurate estimate of the time, cost and resources needed; or if you want better data for project tracking.

Should all the work be identified?

Yes, but not all work has to be detailed in the Planning stage. Planning is ongoing. You should have enough work detailed to provide direction for the first set of deliverables to be created. This ongoing definition of work is called Progressive Elaboration.

Remember to include work for project management deliverables, such as: status reports, team meetings, project communications and ongoing risk management.

Who is best qualified to identify the work?

A team member responsible for completing the work or a subject matter expert is best qualified to identify the work. The Project Manager should not be detailing the work unless they are a subject matter expert. Having the team identify the work is also a great way to build team ownership in the Project Plan.

What is the value of planning to the level of detail of the Work Package?

Work Package definition provides two specific benefits:

Improved accuracy in Planning – estimating project resource requirements, project completion, project costs and identification of risks

Improved tracking during Execution – since work is clearly defined, it is easier to track work completed (compared to the plan) and actual effort (compared to the plan). This way there is early identification of when the project is proceeding as planned; or the project is not going as planned, and adjustments need to be made.

Workshop Idea: Developing Work Packages

Work packages are best created in small teams of individuals responsible for completing the work, or individually for smaller deliverables. If you want to create the work package in a workshop to get better estimates of the work, time and resource require-ments, you should break into small groups that focus on individual work packages, and bring back the results to the entire team for review.

The Project Manager can use this information to secure resources and determine deliverable durations.

Technique: Estimating Effort and Duration

To answer the question, "How long will the work take?" two pieces of data are needed for each work item identified in the Work Package:

- Effort – the amount of time it will take for each team member to complete the work defined without interruption.
- Duration – the amount of effort in relationship to how long it will take to complete the work. Duration takes the effort estimate and creates an updated estimate based on the team

members' availability. For example: if work takes eight hours of effort, but the person assigned to get the work done is only available 50 percent of the time, then the effort is eight hours and the duration is sixteen hours. If five people are in a meeting for one hour, the effort is five hours, the duration is one hour.

Why is effort necessary? Can duration be used instead?

Effort and duration provide very different information. Effort will let you know how much time is required for each deliverable, how many hours you will need for each team member, and define the labor cost associated with creating the deliverable. Duration will let you know how long each team member will need to be available for project work and when the project will be completed. You can determine duration from effort. You cannot always determine effort from duration.

How do I get better estimates?

When it comes to estimating, people are often looking for the magic answer that will let them know exactly how long work will take. No such magic exists. An estimate is a guess. There are ways to improve your guesses—by:

- Using historical data from similar work; this requires capturing actuals from previous projects.
- Having the resource doing the work generate the estimate.
- Utilizing the knowledge of a Subject Matter Expert.
- Piloting or testing a portion of the project, and using the actual efforts and duration for work going forward.
- Creating the work package—the smaller the estimate, the more accurate the estimate.

How accurate are estimates?

Remember that estimates are guesses. Guesses are rarely accurate, but they can be close, or close enough. There are three common types of estimates. Each type of estimate has its own range of accuracy. The common types of estimates and their range of accuracy are:

- **Rough Order of Magnitude (ROM)** estimates can have a margin of error of +/- 25 percent to 50 percent, and are usually developed in the Initiation stage.
- **Budget** estimates are created in the Planning stage with a smaller margin of error, +/- 10 percent to 25 percent.
- **Definitive** or commitment estimates are created from the work package either during the Planning stage or during the ongoing planning that occurs during project Execution. The margin of error for this estimate is +/- 5 percent to 10 percent.

When providing estimates, make sure you clarify whether the estimate you are providing is ROM, budget or definitive.

Work Summary

Ultimately, planning is all about defining the work necessary to create the project (final and interim) and project management deliverables at the level of quality defined in the project requirements. For some deliverables, the work is already known and the planning is simple.
For other deliverables, you will need to ask the following questions, and document the answers in the form of a work package:

- What work needs to be done?
- How long will the work take?
- How many resources do you need to complete the work?
- How will we know when the work is completed?

> *"Plans are only good intentions unless they immediately degenerate into hard work."*
> -Peter Drucker, management consultant, educator and author

Chapter 9: Project Team

> *"Associate with men of good quality if you esteem your own reputation; for it is better to be alone than in bad company."*
> ~George Washington, first President of the United States of America

The human side of a project can be the most difficult. Getting the right support for the project (Chapter 4: Stakeholders) and getting active engagement from the project team is critical to project success.

There are two key pieces of information that anyone working on a project wants to know:

1. What is the project purpose?
2. How do they fit in?

In this chapter, we will review techniques for creating role clarity by defining common project roles and their related responsibilities; on-boarding team members; selecting a team structure; building a positive team by using team building and the stages of team development; and motivating through rewards, recognition and encouraging positive conflict.

Technique: Defining Roles and Responsibilities

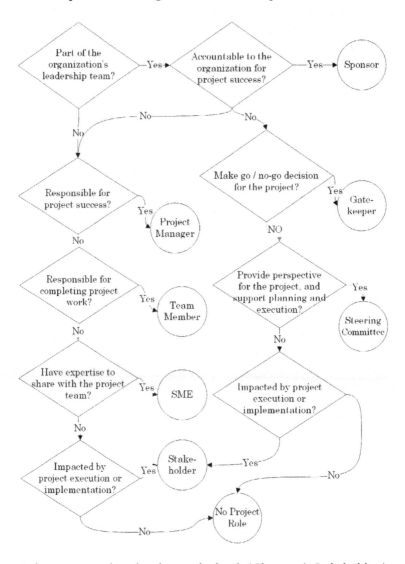

Roles were introduced earlier in the book (Chapter 4: Stakeholders). In this chapter, we will be focusing on role clarity, ensuring that everyone knows what role they play on the project and what is expected from them.

Not all roles are required on every project, and an individual can fulfill more than one role. Project roles can be divided into two categories:

- **Governance** is the structure used within a project environment to make decisions. Governance roles include the Gatekeeper, Steering Committee Member and Sponsor. The Sponsor is the only role that is required on all projects. If there are not Gatekeepers and Steering Committee Members on a project, then the Sponsor assumes their responsibilities.
- **Project Team** is the working component of the project, which includes the roles of Project Manager, Team Member and SME. The minimum required roles for any Project Team are the Project Manager and Team Members.

Let's look at the roles in more detail.

Gatekeeper – The Gatekeeper is a decision maker with the authority to approve, redirect or cancel a project. Gatekeepers are used in large organizations where a single project Sponsor does not have the level of authority necessary to make go/no-go decisions. Specific Gatekeeper responsibilities include:

- Making project decisions for approval, re-scoping or rejection of project approach
- Committing resources and funding to the project
- Working closely with the Sponsor

Steering Committee – The Steering Committee holds the formal ability to exert influence on the project, but is not a decision maker. Steering Committee Members are used in large organizations where a single project Sponsor does not have knowledge of the entire organizational perspective, and representation from different areas are necessary

to steer the project in the best direction for the organization as a whole. Specific Steering Committee responsibilities include:

- Providing cross-functional perspective
- Working closely with the Sponsor
- Providing overall support for project planning and execution

Sponsor – The Sponsor is accountable for enabling project success. The Project Sponsor is the primary benefactor of the project, and works directly to support and empower the Project Manager. The Project Sponsor sets the overall direction of the project, and sets boundaries for project budget, time requirements and acceptance of final deliverables. Sponsor responsibilities include:

- Providing business perspective of the project need and priority
- Defining project success criteria
- Establishing project completion and budget constraints
- Working collaboratively with the Project Manager to document the Project Charter
- Identifying key resources necessary for project planning
- Supporting the collaborative planning process
- Reviewing and approving/rejecting the Project Plan
- Providing ongoing support for project work
- Communicating the continued importance of the project
- Communicating organizational changes that could impact the project
- Communicating with the Steering Committee and Gatekeepers (if they are being used for the project)
- Providing feedback on the project process
- Clarifying critical issues
- Actively supporting the Project Manager and project team
- Supporting project closing activities

- Determining if the project achieved the agreed upon goals
- Willing to integrate organizational changes based on Closing stage learnings

Project Manager – The Project Manager is ultimately responsible for leading the team and meeting the project goals. The Project Manager is responsible for establishing and communicating project goals, scope, work plans, roles and responsibilities, and project risks. The Project Manager is  responsible for establishing the project team, addressing the needs of the team and leveraging individual experiences to enhance team performance. The Project Manager is responsible for communicating project needs and status, throughout the entire organization. Project Manager responsibilities include:

- Clarifying Sponsor expectations
- Working collaboratively with the Project Sponsor to document the Project Charter
- Facilitating the planning process and the application of project management techniques, and ensuring that the right individuals are involved in collaborative planning
- Documenting the Project Plan
- Working with the Sponsor and Key Stakeholders (and Steering Committee and Gatekeepers if utilized on the project) to keep them updated on project progress
- Establishing Management Plans for managing project-related issues, changes, knowledge, quality, risks and communications
- Providing leadership to the project team
- On-boarding team members
- Meeting regularly with the project team to communicate changing priorities, manage issues, resolve conflict and determine project status

- Reviewing and recognizing the contributions of each team member
- Managing risks, issues and project changes
- Keeping project documentation up to date and completing project-related administrative work
- Facilitating the closing process—documenting project lessons learned and best practices
- Willing to integrate changes to the project management process based on the Closing stage learnings

Team Member – The team members are responsible for completing specific project work and adhering to the project approach as documented in the Project Plan. Team member responsibilities include:

- Participating in the collaborative planning process by providing expertise based on past projects and organizational experience
- Identifying the work and estimating effort to complete assigned deliverables
- Identifying and assessing project risks
- Communicating with the Project Manager
- Completing work assignment and producing project deliverables
- Identifying, logging and recommending issue resolutions, using the Issue Management procedure
- Communicating detailed status of work effort on a pre-defined format to the Project Manager
- Implementing approved scope changes
- Participating in the closing process by providing feedback on project process

Subject Matter Expert – The SME provides subject matter expertise based on past projects and organizational experience.

These definitions of roles and responsibilities are based on best practices and years of practical experience. Review the responsibilities and modify them to work effectively within the culture of your organization, and to fit the personalities of the individuals involved in your project. Remember that the only required roles on any project are the Sponsor, Project Manager and Team Members.

There are two common approaches to documenting project roles and responsibilities.

Responsibility Table

This table documents each project role—Sponsor, Project Manager, Team Member—who plays each role, and the responsibilities fulfilled by each role.

Role	Name	Responsibilities
Gatekeeper	Peter Key	• Makes project decisions for approval, re-scoping or rejection of project approach • Commits resources and funding to the project • Works closely with the Sponsor
Sponsor	Mary Sapport	• Accountable for project success • Sets the overall direction, and resolves critical business and project issues • Actively supports the Project Manager

Role	Name	Responsibilities
Project Manager	Jane Charge	• Responsible for project success • Provides team leadership
Team Member	Sam, Bill, Patty...	• Collaborates in project planning • Completes assigned work

RACI

A RACI chart clearly defines project roles and responsibilities for each deliverable within the project scope. Codes are used in the RACI matrix cells to document: Responsible (doer of the work), Accountable (ensures that the work gets done), Consult (has knowledge or information that needs to be included in the creation of the deliverable), Inform (needs information about the status or completion of the deliverable). In a RACI table, only one person should be accountable for ensuring work gets done, an individual can have more than one letter for a deliverable and an individual does not have to have a RACI letter for every deliverable.

	Gatekeeper Peter Key	**Sponsor** Mary Sapport	**Project Manager** Jane Charge	Sam	Bill	Patty
Project Charter	I	A, R	C			
Project Plan	I	I	A, R	C		C
Deliverable A			A	R		
Deliverable B		I	I	R	C	A, R
Deliverable C			I	C	A	R

See Appendix D for an example of a deliverable-based RACI for our sample project: Provide project management training to the entire sales staff, so that the sales team can execute their role as Project Sponsors by end of first quarter 20xx.

Workshop Idea: Establishing Clear Roles and Responsibilities

Two activities that can be completed during a planning workshop to clarify roles and responsibilities are:

1. Reviewing roles and responsibilities—review the roles and responsibilities we've discussed in this text, and make modifications based on your organization. Write each role and each responsibility on individual pieces of paper, and then divide your project team up into small groups. Have the groups mix up the papers and then begin a matching activity where each group does their best to match the responsibilities to each role. After a few minutes of matching, present the solution to the entire team and discuss any difference on how they expect roles and responsibilities to be executed during the project.

2. Building a RACI chart—list all deliverables on the left side of a wall chart, and all project roles (Stakeholders included) across the top of the chart. Populate the RACI by asking a series of questions for each deliverable, and documenting on the chart:
   a. Who does the work? – place an R in the appropriate cells
   b. Who is accountable for getting the work done? – place an A in the appropriate cells

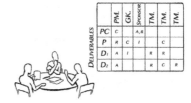

   c. Who should be consulted on the work? – place a C in the appropriate cells
   d. Who should be informed on the progress of the work? – place an I in the appropriate cells

---

Technique: On-Boarding the Team

Many assumptions can be avoided when the project team is fully on-boarded. On-boarding means ensuring that everyone has the same understanding of the project purpose, approach and their role. On-boarding can happen multiple times during the life of the project. The most common times that on-boarding should occur are during:

- Project Planning—to ensure that the core team is fully engaged in the collaborative planning process
- Post Planning, as project Execution begins. This often occurs through a formal "kick-off" meeting that includes:
  - Team Introductions – so everyone knows who is on the team
  - Business Need – so everyone knows why the project is being initiated
  - Project Approach – so that everyone understands the approach that will be used to achieve the project goal (this is especially important for team members that were not involved in the collaborative planning process)
  - Additional Input – it is important that the "kick-off" meeting allows time for team member feedback, ensuring that everyone has an opportunity to contribute at some level to the planning. (If team members have no voice in planning, they may be much less engaged in fulfilling their role in execution.)
  - Establishing Standards and Procedures – so that everyone understands how the team will work together. This can include: status reporting, team meetings, how issues and changes will be handled, and any other policy or procedure that the team needs to be aware of
  - Team Building – to start the project off in a fun and focused way
- Individually, as team members are added to the project.

If on-boarding does not take place, it will take longer for team members to understand the project purpose and their role on the project. On-boarding decreases the time it takes for an individual to become a productive team member.

Technique: Selecting a Team Structure

There are three standard structures used in organizing a project team. Each structure has advantages and disadvantages. If you can, select a structure that provides the best fit for your project. If you cannot select the project structure, then find ways to leverage the advantages and minimize the disadvantages of the structure on your project. The three structures are:

Pure project – in this structure, everyone is assigned to work full time on the project. It is the most powerful structure from a teaming perspective; everyone has a single purpose and a single boss (the Project Manager). Pure project teams can achieve more, faster than any other structure, since they are not distracted by other work going on in the organization. As powerful as this structure is, there may be reluctance for individuals to join a pure project team, unless there is security that there will be another project, or work, remaining post project. It can also be difficult to keep team members on a pure project team towards the end of the project; if they are still concerned about what they will be doing post project, they may be spending time securing the next project to work on.

Functional project – in this structure, the project team is working in a functional area, such as: Human Resources, Finance, Technology, etc. In addition to an individual's role of running the day-to-day operations of the business, they are also assigned to complete project work. This project work is usually functional in nature and managed by the functional manager. The benefit of this structure is that the expertise of the team is high. The disadvantages are that the decisions made on the project are made in functional silos and that running the business usually takes priority over project work.

Matrix project – in this structure, the project team members continue to work in their functional area, completing work to run the business, and are also assigned to work on projects run by a Project Manager that is not within the function. The benefits of a matrix structure include access to experts and cross-functional teams that are less likely to make silo decisions. On the other hand, matrix teams can be the most difficult to lead because the team members report to and are rewarded by their functional manager, and they are still required to complete functional work; therefore, the project manager will often need to negotiate with both the functional manager and the team member to prioritize project work.

Technique: Building and Developing the Team

Volumes of books have been written on teams and team development. I encourage you to read what you can, as the team environment can make or break a project. Over many years of consulting, when I've asked people what makes for an effective team, the following characteristics were cited:

Characteristics of an Effective Team:

- Common Goal
- Clear Role Definition
- Open Communication
- Dedication
- Respect
- Trust
- Support
- Learning Environment

- Common Goal – clear understanding of the project purpose, and how it is aligned and prioritized within the organization

- Clear Role Definition – individuals understand what they bring to the project, and have the skill and ability to execute their responsibilities
- Open Communication – a willingness to share ideas and listen to what others have to say
- Dedication – to the project goals and willingness to do the hard work necessary for project success
- Respect – the team does not have to like each other (although it helps), but everyone should respect the opinions and uniqueness of others
- Trust – the belief that others have the right mix of skills, personal integrity and the willingness to support each other, and that they will follow through on their commitments
- Support – the belief that help is available if needed, and it is okay to provide and seek out support as needed
- Learning Environment – the understanding that perfection is not necessary (even if it may be required at some point in the project); a certain level of imperfection and uncertainty is tolerated on the project as long as the team is learning and improving over time

So how does a group evolve into a team with these characteristics? Sometimes it occurs by happenstance, but more often it happens through intent with the dedicated effort of the Project Manager and the team. In your quest to develop better teams, it is helpful to understand the stages of team development and 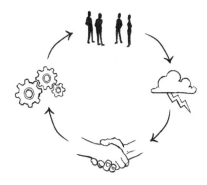 how, as a Project Manager, your leadership style needs to adjust to the stage your team is in.

- Stage I: Forming

As a new team forms, members begin to explore and define the boundaries of acceptable team behavior. This stage begins the transition from a group of indi-  viduals into a team. The Project Manager's leadership style is more directive in a forming team, providing the team members with the information they need to understand the project purpose and their role in it. Then the team can move to the second stage of team development. Team ground rules can be defined to establish agreed upon team behaviors, such as: starting meetings on time, listening to other points of view, staying focused on the task at hand, and sharing ideas openly.

- Stage II: Storming

This is the most difficult stage for the team. In storming, the team members begin to realize that the task at hand may be difficult and time consuming; that the amount of effort required to meet their  objectives may not fit into their originally estimated time frame; and that individuality of the team members may get in the way of achieving the team goals. In this stage of development, the Project Manager needs to modify their leadership style to be more facilitative; allowing individuals to voice their ideas and opinions, making necessary changes to the project approach based on the feedback provided, and protecting team members from any personal attacks (if they occur).

- Stage III: Norming

In this stage, the team members accept the team and the ground rules, and begin to work together to achieve the team objectives. Team members get used to working together; and the individuality of other team members is accepted. In this stage, the Project Manager can rely on traditional management styles to lead a team that understands their roles and that completing the work is necessary for project success.

- Stage IV: Performing

In this stage, the interpersonal issues and distractions of the team have been resolved. The team begins performing. It is in this stage that the team focus is clearly on the steps, processes, tools and techniques required to meet the project goals and objectives. In the Performing stage, the team has reached its full potential to work together. If the team makes it to the Performing stage (not all teams do), then the Project Manager's leadership style needs to move toward coaching and mentoring. Here, the leadership is informally shared as individuals step up to lead based on their individual areas of expertise.

Not all teams make it to the Performing stage. Some teams get stuck along the way. You may have been in a team stuck in the Storming stage, where conflict was the norm for the project—this is not a nice place to be.

Realize that not everyone on the team will transition through the stages at the same time. You can have a team member still unsure of their role—stuck in the Forming stage—while other team members are busy at work in the Norming stage.

Any change that impacts the team can throw the team back to the Forming stage as they struggle to determine if the project goal, approach or their role on the team has changed.

Create a strategy to move your team through theses stages while modeling the characteristics of an effective team.

Team Development Stage	Leadership Style Necessary to Support the Team and Move the Team to the Next Stage of Development
Forming	Directive
Storming	Facilitative
Norming	Supportive
Performing	Coaching and mentoring while encouraging shared leadership

Technique: Motivating the Team with Rewards and Recognition

So, how do you get your project team members engaged and motivated to work on your project? One of the best ways is through motivation. Over the years, I have seen examples that range from great team motivation to total team neglect. Let's look at a couple of examples: one for great team motivation, and another for total team neglect.

An example of positive motivation: I saw a Project Manager provide a Stretch Armstrong doll (a male doll with arms and legs that stretch very far and then reshape themselves) to the team member that stretched themselves the most for the team. The Project Manager required that the current owner of the doll adorn the doll in some way and, within a week or two, give it to another team member that had "stretched themselves" for the project. By the time the project was finished, the doll was wearing a hula skirt, holding a drink umbrella and sitting in a toy lounge chair with tattoos inked on his body. It was a great way to have fun and help the team recognize its own contributions to the project.

On the other extreme: I have talked with team members who, after they rolled off a project, were never told if the project was finished or how the product they created was received in the marketplace. These team members found out by searching the web and reviewing industry articles to see if the project they worked on was launched.

When rewarding and recognizing your team, make sure to leverage any formal processes within the organization, such as feedback on performance reviews and excellence awards.

Informal celebrations are a welcome reward as well, like: team lunches; food at meetings (remember, if your team is not centrally located, to somehow provide food at all locations); and celebrations of specific events, including project milestones and team members' birthdays.

In addition to the formal and informal rewards, make sure you recognize both individual contributions as well as team contributions.

Invest time in getting to know your team. Everyone is a little different in how they like to be motivated, rewarded and recognized.

Technique: Encouraging Positive Conflict

Ah conflict—some people embrace it, while others go out of their way to avoid it. My experience has led me to believe that a dangerous place to be is on a team with no conflict. Without conflict, there can be:

> *"Creativity comes from a conflict of ideas."*
> ~Donatella Versace, Italian fashion designer

- No difference of opinion
- No collaboration
- No innovation
- No uncertainty
- Only suppressed Storming and never Performing

When there is no room for conflict on a team, it can be caused by a dominating team member or Project Manager, or an organizational environment that has artificial harmony. Artificial harmony is when everyone pretends to agree, but does not really agree. When no conflict is allowed, you will see people shutting down, going through the motions or, if they can, exiting the project or the organization.

There are two types of conflict that we are concerned with as a Project Manager:

1. Destructive – when there are personal attacks, limited listening and an unwillingness to compromise, or people are passive aggressive. Avoid this type of conflict.
2. Constructive – when people can share ideas, and challenge thoughts, approaches and roles. With constructive conflict, a team can move toward the Performance stage of team development. Encourage this type of conflict.

Constructive conflict is good.

In order to model constructive conflict, I like to seed a conversation with constructive conflict. By modeling that different perspectives and difficult conversations are welcome, and that individuals will be listened to in a safe environment, it encourages team members to be actively engaged in conversations. I have started meetings and workshops with statements like:

> *"Peace is not absence of conflict, it is the ability to handle conflict by peaceful means."*
> ~Ronald Reagan,
> 40th President of the
> United States of America

- "I have heard in hallway conversations that this project is too big to be successful; that concerns me too. What other concerns do you have?"
- "I drafted a plan, and I am sure it is not perfect. After I review the plan, let's talk about what is wrong with it."
- "This plan looks overly optimistic (or what I call a 'happy plan'). Let's figure out why it will not work, and then modify it to something we all believe in."

Remember, if no one challenges ideas and everyone always agrees, what seems like peace may be artificial harmony. Encourage open and honest conversations, listen non-defensively and allow constructive conflict to be part of the normal behavior for your project team.

Project Team Summary

Successful projects require teamwork. Positive team dynamics start with the Project Manager. As a Project Manager, you should be able to answer these questions positively:

- Does everyone understand their project role?
- Are you building a positive team?

In this chapter, you were provided with a list of project roles and responsibilities, and two approaches to use for role clarity: Responsibility Table and RACI chart.

As a Project Manager, invest time to ensure that you are:

- Selecting the most effective team structure
- Encouraging teamwork
- Building a positive team
- Actively on-boarding team members
- Making time to model the characteristics of effective teamwork
- Paying attention to the stages of team development
- Rewarding and recognizing excellent behaviors
- Encouraging positive conflict on the team

> *"Finding good players is easy. Getting them to play as a team is another story."*
> ~Casey Stengel, American Major League Baseball outfielder and manager

Chapter 10:
Risks

> *"The biggest risk is not taking any risk... In a world that (is) changing really quickly, the only strategy that is guaranteed to fail is not taking risks."*
> ~Mark Zuckerberg, founder of Facebook

Risk is the uncertainty in a project.

Risks are the events we are aware of, but unsure of if and how they may impact the project.

The two questions that risk management helps answer are:

- How much uncertainty on this project is okay?
- How will uncertainty be handled?

All projects have risks. Few Project Managers utilize the strategies necessary to proactively manage risks. In my consulting, I find organizations that identify risks, and react to risks as they occur; but rarely do I see an organization proactively manage risks.

In this chapter, we will begin by covering risk tolerance, ensuring that you have the risk conversation with Key Stakeholders and understand what the appropriate level of risk is for the project. The remaining sections of this chapter will provide you with simple hands-on techniques for identifying, assessing and managing the risks on your project.

Like all techniques we have talked about in this book, the Project Manager is responsible for facilitating the risk management process; but the project team, Sponsor and Key Stakeholders should be involved in the process as well.

Risk Tolerance

Risk tolerance is how much risk is appropriate for the project. Before we talk about tolerance related to the project, let's look at risk tolerance from a personal perspective.

We all have different risk tolerances. There are some people that love uncertainty; they like to try new things. The more uncertainty they have, the higher their satisfaction with what they are doing. These individuals are called Risk Seekers.

Then there is the Risk Adverse—these individuals prefer to work on items that have familiar processes and produce familiar results. They have higher satisfaction when there is little or no risk on a project.

The final category is Risk Neutral—these individuals are not really looking at risks. The level of risk has a minimal impact on what they do or how they approach their work.

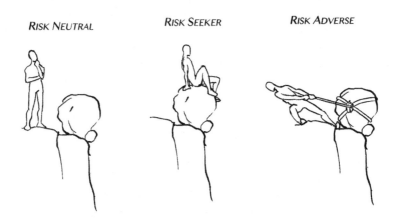

RISK NEUTRAL *RISK SEEKER* *RISK ADVERSE*

So, how would you label yourself: risk seeker, risk adverse or risk neutral? Before you place yourself in a specific category, let's pose two different self-assessments:

1. Review the different scenarios and assess your risk tolerance by checking the option that best describes you:

Scenario	Option A	Option B	Option C
Changing the approach to a project that may cost a little more money than the original budget	☐ Change the approach; what's a few more dollars!	☐ No changes without detailed conversations and agreement by the Sponsor.	☐ If the change will deliver business value, then the money should not be a consideration.

Scenario	Option A	Option B	Option C
Project will complete late	☐ Late is okay, as long as we deliver to the goal.	☐ Do whatever it takes to finish; a commitment is a commitment even if the estimates were wrong.	☐ Just keep working the plan; when it's done, it is done.
Add a resource that is new to the company to your project team	☐ Always willing to on-board new staff. I wonder what skills and experience they have that can be leveraged.	☐ Let's keep the team as is, and only bring in a new resource after they have proven their abilities.	☐ Will only add new staff if we can use them.
Try a new technology to achieve the project results	☐ Yes, I love to try new things.	☐ If we have to use new technology, can we have the old technology available just in case?	☐ New or old, technology makes no difference.

2. Select the answer that best reflects your response to the following questions:

   A. When, in the life of a project, are you more willing to have uncertainty in a project?
      ☐ Early in the life of the project
      ☐ During the middle of the project
      ☐ At project completion
      ☐ Anytime
      ☐ Never

   B. When in the life of a project, would you like the project to be risk free?
      ☐ Early in the life of the project
      ☐ During the middle of the project
      ☐ At project completion
      ☐ Always
      ☐ Never; no risk, no reward

How did you do? In question 1, Option A has answers that a Risk Seeker may select; Option B holds answers that someone who is Risk Adverse may select; and Options C is Risk Neutral. When looking at the scenarios, most people have different levels of risk tolerance. You may have been Risk Adverse when it comes to spending more money, but Risk Neutral when it comes to adding new resources and a Risk Seeker when it comes to trying new technology.

When looking at Questions 2A and 2B, many people have a higher risk tolerance early in the project and a low risk tolerance toward project completion.

The point is we do not always respond the same way to risks. Some risks, we are comfortable with, and we are Risk Seekers; other risks take us out of our comfort zone, and we are Risk Adverse; still, other risks seem to have no impact on us, and we are Risk Neutral.

As a Project Manager, talk with the Sponsor and Key Stakeholders to ensure that everyone agrees on what the risk tolerance should be for the project. The risk tolerance can be higher earlier in the life of the project—this concept is called "front-loading risks." Front-loading risks means to try all the items that might not work early in the life of the project so that you have time to adjust or cancel the project if, in fact, the risks occur.

Workshop Idea: Defining Project Risk Tolerance

In a workshop setting, discussions about risk tolerance are best held following the development of a deliverable-based time line. Once the project time line is established, ask the workshop participants:

- Where in the life of the project should the team embrace risk? Label this portion of the project "Risk Seeker."
- Where in the life of the project should the team minimize risks? Label this portion of the project "Risk Adverse."
- Are there risks in the Risk Adverse portion of the project that can be moved to the Risk Seeker portion of the project?

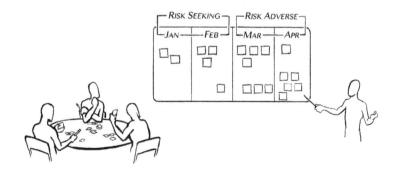

Technique: Identifying Risks

The first step to risk management is to identify all potential events that may occur and could impact the project. When brainstorming risks, think about uncertainty that can be related to technology, project approach, cost, timing, resources and external forces, such as: regulations, vendors, competitors and environmental factors. Each of these categories can be used as a checklist to ensure that you have identified different types of potential project risks.

Risk identification should be completed by the project team. Everyone will bring their own perspective of what risks could occur. Getting the team involved will increase the probability that potential risks are identified.

Risk identification can be completed at various levels of detail:

- At the project as a whole – to identify the uncertainty in the project alignment and approach
- At a specific project phase – to identify the uncertainty by phase
- At the deliverable or major activity level – to identify the uncertainty in individual project components

Risk identification is a great way to engage the naysayers on your project. Leverage the team members that are always eager to tell you what will not work, and harvest their ideas as identified risks.

At the end of brainstorming risks, you should have

Sample: Risk Identification

1. Not enough time to complete deliverables
2. Resources have limited experience and skills
3. Changing priorities of the business
4. Not all requirements have been identified

an extensive list of potential events that, if they do occur, will impact the project. Once you are satisfied with the list of risks (remember, risk management is not a one-time event; you can come back any time in the life of the project to identify new risks), proceed to Step 2: Assessing Risks.

Technique: Assessing Risks

All risks should be evaluated against the:

- Probability that the risk may occur.
- Impact the risk will have on the project if it does occur.

The level of granularity selected to assess risks is up to you. You can use a simple 2x2 matrix, using high and low for probability and impact. Some people like a 3x3 matrix, using high, medium and low to assess probability and impact. You can even go as granular as a 5x5, using a scale of 1–5 for impact; and 90%, 70%, 50%, 30% and 10% for probability. The level of detail depends on your comfort in assessing the risks. I have clients that developed a 10x10 matrix for an even more granular assessment.

I find, as a general rule, individuals who spend a lot of their day analyzing may be more comfortable with the 10x10 or 5x5 matrix. On the other hand, I like to keep my assessment as simple as possible and stick with the 2x2 matrix.

Regardless of what approach you pick to assess risks, each risk will be categorized as either a:

H – High risk
M – Medium risk or
L – Low risk.

Let's look at how the categorization plays out using each of the assessment matrixes:

		Probability	
		High	Low
	High	H	M
Impact	Low	M	L

		Probability		
		High	Medium	Low
	High	H	H	M
Impact	Medium	H	M	L
	Low	M	L	L

		Probability				
		90%	70%	50%	30%	10%
	5	H	H	H	H	M
	4	H	H	H	M	L
Impact 5 – High 1 - Low	3	H	M	M	M	L
	2	M	M	M	L	L
	1	M	L	L	L	L

Sample: After Risk Assessment, each risk should be classified as High, Medium or Low

		Probability	
		High	Low
Impact	High	• Not enough time to complete deliverables • Changing priorities of the business	
	Low	• Resources have limited experience and skills	• Not all requirements have been identified

Assessing each risk gets you ready to move to Step 3: Creating Risk Management Strategies.

Technique: Creating Risk Management Strategies

Finally, we can apply the proactive power of risk management to our project. For each identified and assessed risk, we need to decide if the risk should be:

- Mitigated – adding a proactive strategy, or additional work, designed to either reduce the risk's impact on the project or the probability of the risk occurring
- Have a contingency plan – a backup plan in case the risk occurs
- Have both mitigation and contingency
- Have neither mitigation nor contingency

Risk Terms:

Mitigation: a proactive strategy to either reduce the risk's impact on the project or the probability that the risk will occur

Contingency Plan: a reactive strategy or backup plan in case the risk occurs

Whether you apply any of the above strategies will depend on the risk assessment and the project's risk tolerance. In general:

- High risks (H's in the assessment matrixes) require both mitigation and contingency—a mitigation designed to either reduce the risk's impact on the project or the probability of the risk occurring; and a contingency plan as a backup plan in case the mitigation does not work and the risk occurs.
- Medium risks (M's in the assessment matrixes) require only contingency as a backup plan in case the risk occurs. There is limited value in adding mitigation for a risk that does not have a high probability of occurrence or a high impact on the project.
- Low risks (L's in the assessment matrixes) require neither a mitigation nor contingency. Low risks have both a low probability

of occurrence and a low impact if the risk does occur. Low risks should be documented and watched for just in case their probability or impact increases.

A common error, when new to risk management, is to over mitigate. Remember that mitigation is adding work to the project that would not need to be done if the risk did not exist.

Sample Risk Management Strategies:

Risk	Assessment	Mitigation	Contingency
Not enough time to complete deliverables	High	Add resources	Reduce project scope
Changing priorities of the business	High	Meet with business to create Value Proposition	Cancel or delay project if priority is lowered
Resources have limited experience and skills	Medium	-	Send resources to training
Not all requirements have been identified	Low	-	

All mitigation is work that the project is committing to complete. It is work that is added to the scope of the project. Mitigation could require the addition of a deliverable, changed features to an existing deliverable or work added to the work package. Reconciling the Project Plan with the mitigation strategies ensures that the work, timing, staffing and cost associated with managing the risk is included in the plan.

There are different strategies for risk mitigation; consider:

- Redesigning the project approach to completely avoid the risk. For example, when traveling by car, if the route may get adverse weather with the potential impact on the safety of your travel as well as your arrival time, either:
  - Delay the trip until the forecast predicts better weather, or
  - Take another route
- Transfer the risk to another group by:
  - Having someone else complete the travel, or
  - Using another mode of transportation, ensuring someone else is responsible for the travel safety and timing.
- Accepting the risk when options for mitigation are more unfavorable than letting the risk occur.

The term contingency in project management can have different meanings, depending on the context in which the term is being used, for example:

- **Risk contingency** is the backup plan put in place to react to a risk that has occurred.
- **Cost contingency** is the additional fund held in reserve to be used for unexpected events that are required to be absorbed by the project budget.
- **Time contingency** (also referred to as safety of buffer) is the additional time added to a work package or overall schedule to absorb unexpected work that should have been included in the project schedule.

Contingency should not be used to absorb changes.

Additional Risk Management Topics

Ongoing Risk Management is necessary because risk management is not a one-time event. There will be times within the life of the project that the core team should get back together to review the risk documentation in order to modify the risk assessment with new information and add new risks. Ongoing risk management meetings can be developed as part of the original project schedule. Risk management meetings can occur: at the end of major milestones; between rollouts, waves or iterations; at the completion of a project phase; or as outside changes impact the project strategy.

Residual risk is a term used to assess the amount of remaining risk after high risks have been mitigated. If the mitigations are deemed successful, then the risks can be reassessed as medium risks. The residual risk of a project should be within the threshold of risk tolerance for the project.

Risk triggers are early indicators that a risk is about to occur. The simplest example of a trigger is a traffic light. When the traffic light changes from green to yellow, it is an indicator that the light will soon be red and you will have to stop (or speed up and get through the intersection). The change in light color indicates a change in traffic flow. For your risks, it  may be helpful to identify specific triggers to watch for as an early warning that a risk is about to occur.

Risk reserve is a buffer of time and money held in reserve to absorb a portion of the risk contingency if the risk occurs and the contingency plan needs to be executed. The amount held in reserve is dependent on the probability of the risk, and the time and cost of the contingency. One of our sample risks is that resources have limited experience and skills; it has a low probability (maybe 30 percent) but a high impact. If the risk occurs and resources need to attend training, there will be a week delay in the project. To calculate the risk reserve, multiply the time of the contingency by the probability the risk will occur. In this case, 5 days x 30% = 1.5 days (which we will round up to 2 days). For the financial risk reserve, multiply the cost of two days, or the actual cost of the training, by the probability (30 percent). For example: 5 days of training is $20,000 x 30% = $6,000.

Risk	Assessment	Trigger	Mitigation	Contingency	Residual Risk	Risk Reserve
Resources have limited experience and skills	Medium	Quality of work does not meet requirements	-	Send resources to training	Medium	2 days $6,000

The risk reserve is not enough to cover the entire cost and timing of the contingency, but enough to create a buffer so that if some (not all) of the risks on the project occur, you can absorb the contingency without going back to leadership to ask for more time or money.

Workshop Idea: Managing Project Risks

This risk management activity will be completed in three steps:

- Step 1: Identification – Individually brainstorm the uncertain events that can impact the success of the project. For each risk, document it on a sticky note. Populate as many sticky notes as you can. Resist the urge to analyze and manage the risk; just document as many as you can on the sticky notes.

- Step 2: Assess – Create a 2x2 matrix on a flip chart; label one axis probability and the other axis impact. Have each participant post their sticky notes on the 2x2 risk matrix based on their assessment of the risk. Have all the participants gather near the 2x2 matrix, and review the risks posted in the low probability and low impact area. Remind the team that these risks will get documented, but no additional action will be taken. Next, focus on the high/high risks. Ask each participant to come up and read out loud any risks they posted in the high/high category. If, during this presentation, the team determines that the item is an issue and not a risk, move it to the Issue Log flip chart.

- Step 3: Manage – Focus only on the risks that are assessed as high/high. Have the participants split into small groups. Have each group select the risks that they will work on. For each selected risk, the group will identify an appropriate mitigation strategy (and assign a name to who will be accountable for implementing the mitigation strategy). Remind them that mitigation strategies can include: acceptance of the risk, avoidance of the risk, reducing the impact or reducing the probability. The group will also document a contingency plan for each high/high risk in case the risk occurs. Once the groups are completed with the high/high risks, have them return to the 2x2 matrix and select any additional medium risks that fit in their category (medium risks in the 2x2 matrix are those risks assessed as high/low or low/high). For these risks, the group is to only identify contingency plans and document them on the group's flip chart.

Once the group work is done, have each group report their management strategy for each risk to the entire team.

End the activity with a discussion of the mitigation plans and how they need to be added into the Project Plan.

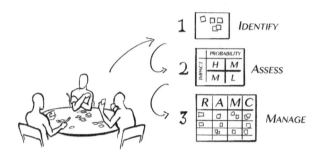

Risks Summary

Risk management answers the questions:

- How much uncertainty on this project is okay?
- How will uncertainty be handled?

Determine the appropriate level of risk tolerance for the project. Remember that risk tolerance can be different for different events or times in the life of the project.

Work collaboratively with the team to complete the risk management process:

1. Identifying potential risks
2. Assessing each risk by probability and impact to categorize each risk as either high, medium or low

3. Creating risk management strategies based on the assessment:
   a. High risks have mitigation and contingency plans
   b. Medium risks have contingency plans
   c. Low risks are documented for awareness

Risk management is not a one-time event. Identify additional times in the life of the project that risks should be reassessed.

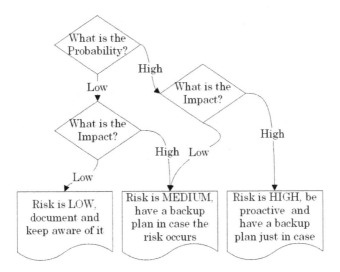

See Appendix D for an example of the Risk Management Strategy for our sample project: Provide project management training to the entire sales staff, so that the sales team can execute their role as Project Sponsors by end of first quarter 20xx.

Any goal worth achieving involves an element of risk.
~Dean Karnazes, Ultramarathon runner,
and author of *Ultramarathon Man:*
Confessions of an All-Night Runner

Chapter 11: Timing

It seems silly to start off by saying all projects take time, but they do.

The most frequently asked question about a project is: how long will the project take? Often followed by: can it be done any faster? In this chapter, we will answer common questions about establishing a project time line and common project management terms, as well as covering techniques for sequencing project work, creating a short-interval schedule, establishing contingency and tracking the schedule.

Let's begin by answering some common questions about project management terms and establishing a project time line.

Who should create the project schedule?

Like most project management techniques, applying the technique is the responsibility of the Project Manager, but should be done with the core project team. Individuals responsible for completing the project work will be committed to a schedule that they had a voice in creating.

What is the best way to create a schedule?

There are many software programs in the marketplace for developing and maintaining a project schedule. For organizations or individuals advanced in project scheduling, any of these tools can provide an excellent solution. My favorite approach is to create a schedule on a whiteboard (or long brown paper on the wall) collaboratively with my project team, and then transfer it to an electronic tool. I post both the photo of the whiteboard and the electronic schedule so individuals can access the format that they find to be most user-friendly.

What is a Gantt chart?

A Gantt chart is the formal name of the graphical representation of the project schedule. It displays deliverables or major blocks of work across time. The chart is named after Henry Gantt, who used the scheduling and other charts in the 1910s for major engineering projects in the United States. See Appendix D for an example of a deliverable-based Gantt chart for our sample project.

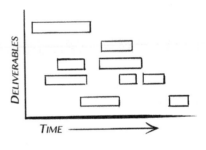

What are milestones?

A milestone is a point in time on a project schedule that indicates when a specific event will occur. Milestones can be used to indicate when work should begin or end for a deliverable, when an event outside the project (that is critical to the project) should be completed, and when key meetings or communication touch points will occur.

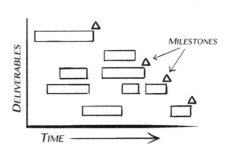

What is critical path?

Critical path is defined as the longest chain of work sequenced by dependences. Critical path is determined by sequencing all work based on work dependencies and then determining the length of the longest path,

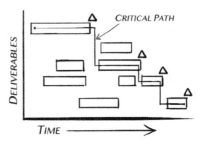

beginning with the first item of work on the project and ending with the last item of work. The critical path defines the earliest that a project can complete (or the shortest project duration). The only way to complete a project sooner than defined by the critical path is to re-scope the project by removing items on the critical path. Critical path can be identified by using the Program Evaluation Review Technique (PERT), which is also called a Network Diagram.

What is a Network Diagram or PERT?

A Network Diagram or PERT is a visual display of either project deliverables or project work organized by finish-to-start dependency. For example, the Network Diagram for the project goal—provide project management training to the entire sales staff, so that the sales team can execute their role as Project Sponsors by end of first quart 20xx—would look like this:

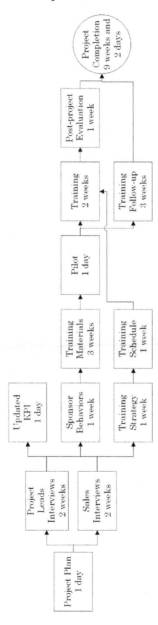

The diagram is created by asking a few questions and documenting the answers visually. The questions are:

- What is the first deliverable that should be created?
- How long will it take to create it (or what is the estimated duration)?
- Once this deliverable is completed, what can be worked on next? And how long will it take to complete?

Continue asking these questions until all project deliverables have been documented in the diagram.

Next, add up all the paths from the first deliverable (Project Plan) to the end of the project (project completion). The longest path will tell you how long the project will take. The longest path is the critical path. Every item not on the critical path contains slack or float.

In the illustration, the following deliverables are on the critical path: Project Plan, Project Manager and sales interviews, sponsor behaviors, training materials, pilot, training and the post-project evaluation. If any of these deliverables take longer to create than planned, it will delay project completion.

What is slack or float?

Slack or float refers to work items or deliverables that are not on the critical path. This means that these items have flexibility in the schedule. They can begin a little early, or a little late, and still not impact the completion date of the project. An item with no slack or float (that is on the critical path) needs to start on time; otherwise, it will jeopardize the project's ability to finish on time.

So how can my project finish faster?

Without banking on a miracle to ensure that the project is done quickly, there are a few things you can try to shorten the duration of a project:

- Remove work from the critical path
- Complete more work in parallel, rather than sequentially (this requires more resources and can increase the project risks)
- Reduce the features/requirements of deliverables
- Invest in innovation during planning to identify non-traditional approaches to complete the project quicker
- Roll out work in phases instead of the traditional "big bang" approach
- Reward the team for early and quality completion of work
- Simplify documentation

Technique: Sequencing Work

Sequencing the work is simply defining when each element of the project will begin and end based on dependencies. There are two situations that can create dependencies:

- Work – the requirement that one item needs to be completed before, after or in some relationship to another item of work.
- Resources – the requirement that an item of work cannot begin until a specific resource is available. Many projects are scheduled based on resource availability because resources are limited.

To determine the sequence of work, it is helpful to understand the different types of work dependencies:

1. Finish to Start – one item must be finished 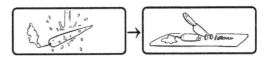 before you can start the next item. For example: vegetables must be cleaned before they are chopped.

2. Finish to Finish – one item must finish before the other item can finish, or two items of work must finish together. For example: all the food cooked for 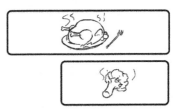 a feast should be finished cooking at the same time.

3. Staggered work is either Start to Finish (one item must start before another item is finished) or Start to Start (an item cannot start until another item is started). For example: once 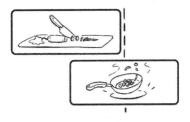 you start chopping the vegetables, you can start sautéing the vegetables.

Here are some common questions and answers about sequencing work and schedule development:

Do you really need to know these different types of work sequencing?

The good news is no! It is important to understand that work can be sequenced in more than one way; work does not always need to be sequential, and it can overlap and be staggered.

When sequencing work, you can begin:

- At project completion, and work backward by asking, "What is the last thing that needs to be done? And what needs to be done before that can begin?" Continue working backward until all the work is scheduled and you have determined when the project should begin to be completed on time.
- At the project beginning by asking, "What is the first thing that should be done? What should be done next?" Continue asking these questions until all work is scheduled and you have determined when the project will be completed based on the start date.

What happens if there is not enough time to complete the project?

When there is not enough time to complete the work defined in the project scope, then the Project Manager needs to first determine why, identify alternative strategies, and then meet with the Sponsor to discuss options and make a decision for going forward. Understanding the cause of "not enough time" will help you identify alternatives for moving forward. Common alternative strategies can include:

- Reducing the scope of the project (in terms of the quantity of deliverables or the requirements that must be met for each deliverable)
- Adding more resources (this is not always the solution; studies have illustrated that adding more resources can actually slow down project work)
- Increasing the risk tolerance of the project by trying more uncertain approaches, hoping they will work and that the project will finish sooner; but also realizing that the increased risk may cause the project to not finish on time, on budget or on performance
- Phasing in project deliverables (maybe a 70 percent solution can be delivered on time, and then the remaining

30 percent, if still needed, can be added later in another phase)

- Buying an existing deliverable instead of building the deliverable

At what level of detail should the schedule be developed?

Start with a high-level schedule based on the deliverables defined in the scope statement. Be careful not to get into the details of the schedule too soon. If you attempt to create a perfect schedule at the lowest level of work early on in the project, every time there are small changes in the project timing or resources, you will have to update the schedule. So, keep the schedule at the phase and deliverable level—we can call this the high-level schedule or master schedule. When working on the details during project execution, use the technique, developing a short-interval schedule, explained later in this chapter.

The high-level schedule provides enough information to determine when:

- Work on each project deliverable will begin and end
- Resources are needed, based on the deliverables they will be working on

What is the ideal duration of a deliverable listed on a project schedule?

The duration of each deliverable on the high-level schedule should be determined by the amount of work (defined in the work package) and the availability of resources. That said, I recommend that deliverables over a month in duration be broken down into smaller components so that there is a clear understanding of when an item is complete. For example, when tracking a deliverable that will take three months to create, it is easy to state that the deliverable is being worked on, but harder to determine if the deliverable will be completed on time. If this same deliverable is broken down into three components, and each component scheduled sequentially, then each month, you will be able to know, with accuracy, when each third of the total deliverable will be completed.

How do resources impact the schedule?

When creating the high-level schedule, check with each resource to ensure they are available when the deliverables they will be working on are scheduled to be created. Don't assume resources are available based on your schedule—they probably have other commitments vying for their time. When schedules are created collaboratively, you have buy-in during schedule development from the committed resources.

Also, if you schedule a person to work forty hours in a week, realize that it will require them to work more than a traditional work week. Resources probably have other standing commitments (meetings, training, supporting activities). In organizations that follow Lean Manufacturing processes, they only schedule resources for 80 percent of their available time, leaving 20 percent for unforeseen events.

Workshop Idea: Creating the Project Schedule

Create a time line on a wall chart labeled with the beginning and ending project dates; then, have the workshop participants brainstorm all the deliverables and major activities that must be completed to achieve the project goal, and document them on individual sticky notes.

Have the workshop participants place the sticky notes on the time line under the month that activity will occur.

Once all the sticky notes are posted, have the entire team stand around the time line while each participant presents the activities and deliverables they posted on the time line. Encourage conversation so that new items are discovered and added to the time line as necessary.

End the activity with a discussion to gain buy-in on the project schedule from all participants.

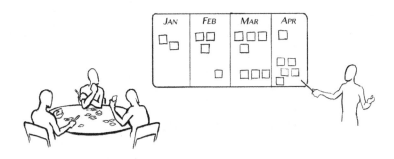

Technique: Developing a Short-Interval Schedule

Short-interval scheduling is exactly as it sounds: over short periods of time, you create the detailed schedule by focusing on the work and resources necessary to complete the work. You will need to determine, based on your experience, what you define as a short period of time. If you work in a:

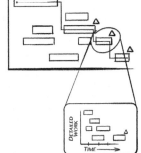

- Stable environment—where resources, once committed, will be available; and the scope of the project is accepted, and changes will occur following a regularly scheduled process—then the short-interval you define may be weeks or even a month.

- Always changing environment—where resources can change frequently, work is not well defined, and changes can occur frequently—then the short-interval you define may be days or weeks.

Once you determine the duration of the short-interval, then either use the work package already defined for the deliverable or define the work necessary to be completed during the short-interval. Make sure when developing the short-interval schedule that you are meeting the completion dates established in the high-level schedule.

Technique: Establishing Contingency

The definition of contingency is: additional buffer in your project that is used to absorb the things you did not know you did not know about (sometimes called the "unknown unknowns"). If you know exactly how much time is needed for project work, then you will not need contingency. If, on the other hand, you are only guessing what the project work, effort and who the available resources are, then some contingency should be added. The amount of contingency you add is based on your level of confidence in the project estimates. If you have a good history and a detailed, collaboratively

Schedule contingency (also referred to as safety or buffer) is the additional time added to a work package or overall schedule to absorb unexpected work that should have been included in the project schedule.

Schedule contingency is *not* the same as risk contingency or cost contingency.

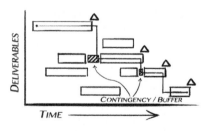

built plan, then a small contingency of 5 percent to 20 percent might be sufficient. If you have no history with similar projects and have not developed a detailed plan, then a much higher contingency might be more realistic. Use your experience and your confidence in the details of you Project Plan to determine how much contingency is necessary.

The terms contingency, safety and buffer are often used interchangeably.

Here are some common questions and answers about the use of contingency:

Where does contingency get added to the schedule?

There are a few good locations for adding contingency to the schedule:

- In the work package for each detailed deliverable – determine how much schedule contingency should be added for each deliverable and place it in the work package for that deliverable. This way, contingency can be tracked at a deliverable level by adding as much or as little as needed.
- At project completion – add contingency at the end of the project, and use the new end date as your commitment date. For example, if the project is scheduled for thirty days, and your level of confidence in meeting that date is high, you can add one day of buffer/contingency and commit to completing the project on day thirty-one, but build your schedule to take the planned thirty days.
- Any time a non-critical path activity leads into the critical path.

How do you communicate the use of contingency?

This is a tricky question. Sometimes you can talk about contingency: why it is in the Project Plan and what it will be used for. Other times, contingency is thought of as a bad word used to buffer your project so you don't have to work very hard, or so that you can get non-project related work done during the project or because you don't want to make a commitment. Openly having contingency in a project requires a level of trust between the Project Manager and the Sponsor—enough trust that the Project Manager can admit there are items they don't know they don't know about (one definition of contingency) and that they are willing to discuss them openly.

I always recommend sharing the contingency information: where it is in the schedule, what it will be used for and what happens if it is not needed (early completion). If you are in an environment where these conversations cannot happen, unfortunately, you will still need contingency in your project. Project Managers have come up with many creative approaches to hiding contingency in the schedule when it cannot be discussed.

Whatever approach you select, just remember that the best way to build trust is to deliver to your commitments in a way that builds positive relationships.

Why add contingency; doesn't work just expand to fill the time available?

There is a management philosophy that believes that work will expand to fill the time available; and there is truth to this thought. If the reward for early completion is more work, then it is more likely work will expand to fill up the time available. If the reward for early completion is the ability to work on special projects, coaching, training or even time off, then work, when possible, will complete early.

Look at the rewards structure in your organization. How are people rewarded for early completion? This might help you understand when contingency will be taken advantage of or used as intended.

Technique: Tracking the Schedule

A high-level schedule that is deliverable based is easy to track. When tracking the project, consider the following:

- Capturing actual efforts to determine progress to date as well as provide valuable information for planning similar projects in the future.
- Reconciling the short-interval schedule to ensure that milestones for deliverable completions are met.
- Updating the short-interval schedule for the next iteration of work.

When the actuals captured are different from the estimated efforts and durations established in the Project Plan, consider:

- The reasons that the actuals are different than planned.
- How the actuals will impact the remainder of the project in terms of timing, resource requirements and cost.

If you learn while tracking actuals that the projections at completion are different than planned, this should trigger a conversation with the Sponsor and Key Stakeholders. The purpose of this conversation is to determine if the new projections impact the Business Case and the financial justification of the project. It is acceptable to cancel or re-plan a project when projections after the project begins redefine what it will take to complete the project.

When tracking the project time, remember that it is only one component of the project. Tracking the project financial and deliverable completion should be considered when analyzing project progress.

Timing Summary

Developing the project schedule helps to answer: How long will the project take?

When creating the project time line, remember to:

- Challenge dependencies—deliverables and work can be sequenced in more than one way; work does not always need to be sequential, it can overlap and be staggered.
- Start with a high-level schedule based on the deliverables defined in the scope statement. Be careful not to get into the details of the schedule too soon.
- Check with each resource to ensure that they are available during the time that the deliverables they will be working on are scheduled to be created. Don't assume resources are available based on your schedule—they probably have other commitments vying for their time.
- Create a detailed short-interval schedule that meets the completion dates established in the high-level schedule.
- Use your experience and your confidence in the details of you Project Plan to determine how much contingency is necessary. Place contingency in the work package, or at project completion or any time a non-critical path activity leads into the critical path.
- When tracking the project time, remember that it is only one component of the project. Tracking the project financial and deliverable completion should be considered when analyzing project progress.

> *"The key is not to prioritize what's on your schedule, but to schedule your priorities."*
> ~Stephen Covey, educator, author and
> keynote speaker

Chapter 12: Communication

> *"The single biggest problem in communication
> is the illusion that it has taken place."*
> –George Bernard Shaw, Irish playwright

Project Managers spend a significant amount of their time ensuring that everyone has a common understanding of the project's purpose, approach and progress. Actively managing communications answers the following questions:

- Who needs information on the project?
- What do they need to know?
- When do they need information?
- How will they get the information?

Communication is a critical, yet difficult part of any project. From my experience, I have learned that just because you say something, it does not mean the other person heard or understood you. The classroom provides a perfect example of the challenges in delivering effective communications. For instance, when I set up for any activity, I model the activity on a whiteboard first, and then provide both written and oral directions, including a sample or a template.

In every case, at least one student will ask me or a peer, "What is the activity?" Is the model fuzzy? Are the directions inadequate? Are the samples and templates worthless? They may not be perfect, but they are pretty good; plenty good enough to provide the information needed. So, what went wrong? What can you do to improve the probability that communications will be effective?

In this chapter, we will cover considerations for targeting communications and techniques for building a communication plan, developing status reports as well as scheduling team meetings.

Communication Considerations

Think of communications like a mini project. When preparing to communicate, ask yourself the same types of questions that you should when organizing a project, such as:

- What is the goal of the communication?
- How will you know when the communication is successful?
- What is the best way to deliver the message?
- What uncertainty exists that may impact the success of the communication?
- How long should the communication take?

Having clear answers to these questions will improve the effectiveness of your communications. In addition, consider the following when developing your communications.

- **Provide a clear message** – know the purpose of your communication, and state it clearly. Make it easy for the audience of your message to understand what you want them to know. Is the purpose of the communication to inform, gain support or make a decision? Don't keep the audience guessing. If you do, you will lose the audience.

- **Know your audience** – understand the biases and preference of the audience. When you think about the audience, make sure you are focusing on what they need to know, not what you want to say (they are not always the same thing). Provide enough information for the audience—if they like details, provide them with details; if they like summary, then provide a summary. Take time to understand your audience, and provide information from an audience-focused perspective.

- **Pick the right media** – it seems the default is always e-mail (people like the documentation it provides). But e-mail is not always the best way to communicate. Face to face is still the best approach to gaining understanding. I realize it is not always possible, but invest time in face to face when you can. Use other mediums of communication—texting, instant messages, electronic portals (web pages, shared drives, SharePoint), meetings, presentations and videos—as appropriate for both the content you need to share as well as the preference of your audience.

- **Use a multi-pronged approach** – there are many events fighting for our attention. Hearing something one time is rarely enough to engage. Sending out a mass e-mail is likely to get it deleted or filed away, but rarely read. I am guilty of checking my e-mails after a day on the road and making three passes: first deleting, filing others for maybe later reading, and then finally reading the e-mails that remain. I am sure that everyone who sends an e-mail assumes (or hopes) that their e-mails are being read. Marketers use the "rule of seven": a customer has to have seven interactions with a product before they are likely to make a purchase. How many times does someone need to hear about your project before they understand it? More than once, closer to seven? So, when communication is important, create a multi-pronged approach: talk about it at a meeting, send a reminder e-mail, put up posters in your workspace . . . Be creative, you are fighting for the attention of your audience.

- **Listen** – communication is a two-way process; listening is as important as, or may be more important than speaking. The ancient philosopher Epictetus said it best when he said, "We have two ears and one mouth so that we can listen twice as much as we speak." It is in listening that we learn. So, invest time in the project to listen to the expectations, needs and ideas of others.

Technique: Building the Communication Plan

A communication plan is a simple technique that is not used often enough. A Project Manager is a planner by discipline, but communication is often left to happenstance, or to the optimistic thought that team meetings and status reports will provide all the necessary information.

When I facilitate post-project evaluations, the most common response I hear is, "No one told me" or "I didn't know." The bottom line is that not enough of the right kind of communication is occurring on projects.

The communication plan is focused on who needs information and what information they need (as opposed to what information the Project Manager thinks should be shared—just in case the Project Manager is not all-knowing). The communication plan is created by answering a series of questions and documenting them in a simple table. Begin by asking:

- **Audience** –Who needs information on the project? Brainstorm all individuals that need information on the project. This list should include already identified individuals like Stakeholders and project team members, as well as anyone else inside or outside the project and organization that will need information on the project.

- **Content** – What do they need to know? For each individual, figure out what information they need. When we send unnecessary information to people, we may condition them to not read or listen to what we have to say. Make sure the information provided is audience focused. One size does not fit all. If the audience is the Sponsor, Steering Committee, Gatekeeper or other Key Stakeholders, review their success criteria (or KPIs) to see if you can provide information that is aligned with their priorities.

- **Timing** – When do they need information? Timing can be either:
  - Event driven – triggered by the arrival of an event (e.g., thirty days prior, the day of, the day after)
  - Time driven – triggered by the passage of time (e.g., every day, every week, once a month)

Make sure the timing selected is driven by the information needs of the audience and the availability of data (no need to report costs weekly when the information is only available monthly).

- **Medium** – How will they get the information? Match the medium used to deliver the information to the audience's preferences. Don't expect everyone to have the same availability to technology that you have. There are some people that are still on non-supported versions of software (so, don't create files they cannot open), and even some that do not have cell phones (so, don't send them text messages). Again, you need to be audience focused. When developing communications, consider both a push and pull approach. Push is providing the same information in a standard way to everyone; for example, sending documentation, giving a presentation or attending a meeting to provide information. Pull is making the information available for the audience to get when they have time, or are interested in getting the information; for example, posting information to a shared drive, website or SharePoint. Remember that face to face is still the most effective medium, so use it as often as you can.

- **Responsible** – Who will provide the communication? Look at each communication individually and determine who is in the best position to share the information. Then, make them responsible. Not all project communications should come from the Project Manager. The Sponsor, Key Stakeholders and even team members can be responsible for project communications. Use the communication plan to:
  - Build opportunities for team members. If a team member would like exposure to someone in the organization, then make them responsible for communicating to them, and coach them to increase their success.
  - Leverage existing relationships. If a team member has a strong relationship with a Key Stakeholder, then they may be the best candidate to deliver the communication.

- **Feedback** – How will you know the communication was received as intended? Just because you told them, it does not mean that they understand the information. Look for ways to gather feedback to validate if the communication was received as intended. Some communications have feedback imbedded in the communications. For example: if you ask for an RSVP, or a decision or specific action, you can observe and see if the action occurs—validation that the message was received. Other communications will require follow up by you to ensure that the message was received. For example: if you send out an e-mail and then follow up with a phone call a few days later to see if there are any questions, you will find out if the e-mail was read and if the information was understood.

Audience (Who)	Content (What)	Timing (When)	Medium (How)	Responsible	Feedback
Project Managers, Sales Staff and Sales Managers	Need for training	At project kick-off	Face to face	PMO (Sponsor)	Commitment to attend training
	Interview schedule	At project kick-off	Face to face	Training (Project Manager)	Accept interview meeting notice
	Defined Sponsor Behaviors	Post interviews	Webinar	PMO (Sponsor) and Training (Project Manager)	-
	Follow-up sessions	At training	Face to face	Training (Project Manager)	Attendance
	Project Evaluation	At project completion	Webinar	Training (Project Manager)	-
	Training schedule	At project kick-off	E-mail	Training (Project Manager)	Accept training notification

Audience (Who)	Content (What)	Timing (When)	Medium (How)	Responsible	Feedback
PMO	Project Plan	mm/dd/yy	Face to face	Training (Project Manager)	Approval
	Training Plan	mm/dd/yy	Face to face	Training (Project Manager)	Approval
	Status	Every other week	E-mail	Training (Project Manager)	-
	Project Evaluation	At project completion	Webinar	Training (Project Manager)	-

Here are some common questions and answers about project communications:

Why do I need a Communication Plan; we already have team meetings?

> Team meetings and status can be an effective way to share some communications; but, stakeholders are usually not included in either of these mediums. Also, team meetings and status are usually used for status information; there may be other ideas that need to be communicated. I recommend that you create the communication plan first; if after creating the plan, you determine that the only communication necessary can occur in team meetings and status, you are fine. However, I will be surprised if you don't identify some previously overlooked communications.

What is the best approach to getting your information across?

Wouldn't it be great if there was one best way to get all information across? There are as many best ways as there are audiences and content. And that might be the closest answer—the best approach to getting information across is to target it to the audience and the content.

Why is it so difficult to gain a common understanding? Or why is effective communications so difficult?

The answer in one word is "filters." We all have filters that affect the way we hear and understand things. Filters can be existing knowledge, past experiences and personal biases, just to name a few. For example:

If you and I think alike, and have had positive experiences listening to each other in the past, then we are more likely to listen to each other in the future. On the other hand, if I tell you about something you already know, your mind may wander off, and you will be less likely to listen to (or read) what I have to share.

If two people often disagree, they will be less interested in each other's opinions.

If I meet someone new, my mind will most likely be busy doing a quick assessment of whether or not that person is a creditable source before I will begin to truly hear what they have to say.

Filters are a critical component of communication. Take time to understand your audience before you communicate so that you target your message, medium and delivery to the given audience's filters.

How can I tell when a communication is effective?

A communication is effective when the communication objective is achieved. This means you must:

- Know the point of your communication before you begin (don't just talk to fill up time, or type to fill up space).
- Gather feedback to validate that the communication was received as intended.

Feedback is built into some communications; for example, presenting a Project Plan to the project Sponsor should end with approval to more forward, modify or cancel the project. All of these options provide clear feedback on the communications. If clear feedback is needed and not part of the normal communications, ask open-ended questions (questions that cannot be answered with a yes or no) to ensure that the communication objective has been achieved.

My team is geographically diverse (all over town, or all over the world), so how should I communicate?

You need to invest more time in communications when working with teams that are not physically in the same place. A communication plan is critical for success in a graphically diverse team. One recommendation is to schedule more frequent, briefer conversations. Another recommendation is to put a "twist" on the communication plan by creating a plan that is focused on the project team. In these situations, everyone creates a communication plan for themselves by placing their name in the audience column, and then defining what information they need, when they need it, how they need it and who should provide it. It is a powerful exercise that will highlight just how much communication needs to occur for team members to be informed.

Workshop Idea: Developing a Communication Plan

Create a Communication Plan template on a wall chart, labeling the columns with: Who, What, When, How, Responsible and Feedback.

Begin by having the workshop participants identify all the individuals or groups that will need information on this project. Write each individual or group on a sticky note, and post them on the wall chart under the column labeled Who.

Review the Stakeholders list, if they are not included in the sticky notes on the Who column, add them to the wall chart.

Next, divide the workshop participants into small teams, and distribute the Who sticky notes evenly between the teams. For each Who, have the teams identify:

- What they need to know
- How often they need to know it
- How that information will get to them
- Who is responsible for communicating this information

Have each team share their Communication Plan with all the participants for questions and buy-in.

COMMUNICATION PLAN

Technique: Developing Status Reports

Status reports are a traditional byproduct of a project. They are created by the Project Manager to keep
others informed on what is going on with the project.
A traditional status report includes: work completed,
financial spending, high-level issues and risks, and
planned activity for the next reporting period. This

information is most interesting and understood by the Project
Manager, and can be very boring for the intended audience. Creating
project status for the sake of status is a waste of time and resources.
Status reports must provide value for the intended audience, not just
the Project Manager or project team.

The discipline of project management has come a long way in creating a more graphical representation of project status. These graphic
charts are better positioned to communicate trends over time (an
increase or decrease in the number of issues or risks).

When beginning a project, sit down with the Sponsor and Key
Stakeholders, and draft out the information that they would like to
see on a status report. Follow the communication plan format by
asking: what do you want to know, how often do you want to know,
how do you want to receive the information, who should provide
the different pieces of information and how will they provide the
Project Manager with feedback to validate that the status report is
adding value? This will aid you in creating a valuable status report
that is focused on the key items of interest to the Sponsor and Key
Stakeholders.

As an example: I ran a project for a client who was only concerned
with getting the work done and achieving regulatory compliance.
They were too busy to complete the work in house, so I stepped in
and ran the project. We created an approach where small components were completed sequentially. Each component was reviewed

for and passed regulatory compliance before it was completed. The status report became a simple statement of the components completed that met regulatory compliance, nothing else. It was simple to create, and met the needs of the client.

Status reports can have standard components, but should be graphical in nature and aligned with the success criteria of the Sponsor and Key Stakeholders.

Technique: Scheduling Team Meetings

Just the thought of a team meeting is enough to make a lot of people run in the opposite direction. Team meetings can be the most boring meetings—listening to everyone share their progress as you try to stay awake while waiting for your turn. There must be a better way, and there is. Let's move away from the standard weekly one-hour meeting and schedule team meetings based on the communication plan and the current cadence of the project. There are times when meetings should be:

- Five-minute stand-up meetings (attributed to Agile Project Management approaches) – they consist of holding brief daily meetings where everyone shares what they are working on and if they need assistance (if assistance is needed, it is handled outside of the stand-up meeting).
- Technique-focused meetings; for example, meetings to reassess project risks, or update the communication plan or solve a specific problem.
- Ongoing planning meetings for the next phase of a project.
- One-hour standard meetings – to review individual progress in detail.
- Canceled if little progress needs to be shared.

Run the team meeting like a little project. Be sure to create an agenda and define:

- The meeting purpose – meeting goal and desired outcome
- Meeting participants (not every team member needs to come to every meeting)
- Discussion items (this is like a work package for the meeting that lists all discussion topics, who will lead each topic and how much time will be dedicated to the topic)
- Meeting timing – based on how much time will be dedicated to each topic
- Follow-up items and next steps

Let the meeting agenda dictate the duration of the team meeting.

Communication Summary

Effective communication is critical to project success. Communication should be done with intent, not by happenstance.

When preparing to communicate, ask yourself:

- What is the goal of the communication?
- How will I know when the communication is successful?
- What is the best way to deliver the message?
- What uncertainty exists that may impact the success of the communication?
- How long should the communication take?

Having clear answers to these questions will improve the effectiveness of your communications. In addition, consider the following best practices when developing your communications.

- Provide a clear message
- Know your audience
- Pick the right media
- Use a multi-pronged approach
- Listen

Build a communication plan by answering a series of questions and documenting them in a simple table. Begin by asking:

- Who needs information on the project? – to define the audience
- What do they need to know? – to determine the content
- When do they need the information? – to determine the timing
- How will they get the information? – to determine the medium
- Who will provide the communication? – to determine who is responsible
- How will you know the communication was received as intended? – to determine the feedback loop

Develop targeted status reports that are graphical in nature and aligned with the success criteria of the Sponsor and Key Stakeholders.

When scheduling team meetings, be sure to be flexible about when they are scheduled. Create an agenda before the meeting and define:

- The meeting purpose – meeting goal and desired outcome
- Meeting participants (not every team member needs to come to every meeting)
- Discussion items (this is like a work package for the meeting that lists all discussion topics, who will lead each topic and how much time will be dedicated to the topic)
- Meeting timing – based on how much time will be dedicated to each topic
- Follow-up items and next steps

Let the meeting agenda dictate the duration of the team meeting.

*"It usually takes me more than three weeks to
prepare a good impromptu speech."*
-Mark Twain, American author and humorist

Chapter 13: Financing

"*Time is money.*"
~Benjamin Franklin, Founding Father
of the United States of America

Every project has a cost. Not all projects have budgets. In fact, only a small percentage of companies I work with create and track budgets for their projects. The cost of a project is one side of the project constraint triangle. Without considering the financial impact of a project, one side of the triangle is missing (this can make defining and managing scope challenging when all work is considered free).

Determining project financials answers the questions:

- What needs to be bought?
- What will the project cost?

In this chapter, we will review techniques for making a buy or build decision, developing a project and lifecycle budget, and for tracking actual project costs, including earned value.

Technique: Making a Buy or Build Decision

When developing the project approach, and defining the project deliverables, there may be some deliverables the team will decide to create and some deliverables that the team will decide to purchase. When making a buy or build decision, take the following items into consideration:

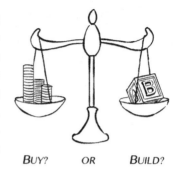

BUY?   OR   BUILD?

- Project time commitment – will buying or building support the project timing?
- Project cost – will buying or building support the project budget?
- Deliverable requirements – which approach will more likely deliver to the level of quality defined by the Sponsor and Key Stakeholders, buying or building?
- Resource availability and skills – do the resources available have the time and the skills necessary to build the deliverables to the requirements within the schedule defined for the project?

Some buy versus build decisions are easy:

- Should you buy or build the freezer necessary to store the ice cream at the desired level of coldness? Obviously, buy (unless you have freezer building expertise).
- Should you buy or produce the raw ingredients necessary to follow the ice cream recipe? Some ingredients might be easily grown if you have a plot of land; other ingredients will be better to buy (unless you have dairy cows).

Some buy versus build decisions are more difficult; for example: should you create a new recipe or purchase the recipe from the closed ice-cream store down the street that has historical significance and a following in your home town?

If your organization has a procurement department and you made the decision to buy deliverables, make sure you work with procurement to complete the selection process and secure the deliverables.

Technique: Establishing a Project Budget

This technique is meant to provide you with a broad understanding of the items that should be considered when developing a budget. For specific financial information, it is recommended that the Project Manager work closely with an individual from your company's finance department to ensure that your budgeting approach is aligned with the company's.

Once estimates of time and resource requirements have been completed in the Project Plan, the budget can be developed. The budget documents the project costs.

Budgets can be developed for each deliverable or for the entire project. When developing the budget, costs can be divided into two categories:

- Expenses, which can include:
  - Labor – the cost of securing the project team. Labor is calculated by the number of estimated effort hours for each resource multiplied by the loaded cost of each resource (or average fully loaded labor cost).
  - Materials – the cost of any materials necessary to complete the project (this can include printing and mailings).

- ○ Consulting/Vendor – the cost of any consulting or vendor fees necessary to complete the project.
- ○ Travel – the cost of any travel necessary to complete the project (this includes airfare, lodging, meals, mileage reimbursement, etc.).
- ○ Training – the cost associated with any training of the project team necessary to complete the project.

- • Capital, which can include:
  - ○ Equipment – the cost of purchasing any new equipment (including machinery and computer hardware) necessary to complete the project.
  - ○ Facilities – the cost of acquiring or updating any physical facilities necessary for the completion of the project.
  - ○ Software – the cost of purchasing new software necessary for the completion of the project.

Budgets should be either time based or deliverable based, so that you can compare planned spending or expenses to actual spending or expenses. A time-based budget could look like this:

Budget Category	Period 1	Period 2	Period 3	Totals
Labor	50,000	75,000	60,000	185,000
Materials	0	10,000	5,000	15,000
Consulting	20,000	5,000	10,000	35,000
Travel	5,000	5,000	7,500	17,500
Training	10,000	0	0	10,000
Equipment	0	150,000	8,000	158,000
Facilities	0	0	0	0
Software	0	0	0	0
Total	85,000	245,000	90,500	420,500

A deliverable-based budget could look list this:

Deliverable	Expense	Capital	
Project Management	50,000		
Design	100,000		
Training	10,000		
Pilot	15,000		
Equipment		158,000	
Construction	17,500		
Test	35,000		
Implement	35,000		
Total	262,500	158,000	420,500

Here are some common questions and answers about budgeting for your project:

Does every project require a budget?

> This is really an organizational culture question. If your organization requires a budget, the answer is an easy yes. If your organization does not, then that is one less thing for a Project Manager to worry about. I recommend creating a budget because a budget establishes value for the Project Manager; it is a metric that can determine if the work dedicated to the project is worth the reward the project will generate.

Why should I create a budget if I am not really spending any money?

> You may not be required to pay anyone for their work, or purchase any items that require you to spend money, but there is still a cost associated with the project. Running a project without a budget is like building a house without a budget. Wouldn't that be fun? You could add anything you wanted and not worry

about how much it cost. Since, in the real world, you have to pay for what is included in the house being built, you prioritize what is important and only include those items you can afford. A project should be thought of in the same way as the house example. If there is no thought to the cost of a project, the scope can increase beyond what is necessary to achieve the project goal.

Are all budgets equal?

All budgets should be equal if they include the "all in" cost of completing a project. Before you compare the budget on two projects, or two project approaches, complete a little due diligence to determine if the budgets are equal. Some items to look for in budgets to understand what is included or excluded are:

- Does the budget only include out-of-pocket expenses? – items you will actually pay for
- Does the budget include internal labor costs? – usually an average fully loaded rate that takes into consideration salaries and benefits (not the actual salary of the project team)
- Does the labor cost include all labor; including the cost of the project team as well as the Sponsor and Key Stakeholders that may invest significant time in the project?

Who creates the budget?

The Project Manager is responsible for the creation of the budget based on the Project Plan and executing the project within this budget. The budget should be created within the tolerance of the financial threshold created in the Project Charter and established by the Sponsor. If the project approach pushes the budget beyond this threshold, then a conversation should be held between the Project Manager and the Sponsor, and the Business Case should be reevaluated to see if the project is still viable, given the newest budget estimates.

How is the budget tied to the Project Plan?

> The budget should *not* be created in a vacuum. It should be based on the estimates documented in the Project Plan; specifically, the work package that details how much estimated effort and resources are needed to complete each deliverable. The budget should include the cost of resources, the cost of all risk mitigation and have a risk buffer to manage some of the risk contingency that might be needed.

What is financial contingency; and do I need it in my budget?

> Contingency is an additional financial buffer in your project that is used to absorb the cost you underestimated or did not know about (similar to schedule contingency, but now with a focus on costs). If you know exactly how much money is needed for your project, then you will not need contingency. If, on the other hand, you are only guessing what the project cost will be, then some contingency should be added. The amount of contingency you add is based on your level of confidence in the project estimates.

Workshop Idea: Establishing a Project Budget

A budget is best created by the Project Manager and representation from the financial department. If you would like to create the budget during a planning workshop, it is recommended that the budget be created toward the end—after deliverables, resources, timing and risks have been identified. Have the workshop participants identify potential areas of cost for the Project Manager and finance department representative to use to build out the budget while the rest of the team is working on other techniques (such as building out the communication plan). The budget can then be reported back to the workshop participants.

Even if the budget will not be established during the planning workshop, the team should still highlight potential areas of cost for the Project Manager to use when it's time to create it.

Technique: Developing a Lifecycle Budget

This technique provides highlights of a lifecycle budget. As in the previous technique, it is recommended that the Project Manager work closely with finance to ensure that you are following company policy.

The lifecycle budget documents the estimated one-time project costs (project budget) as well as ongoing costs and revenue generated by the project. The lifecycle budget includes:

- One-time project costs – the budgeted amount for the project.
- Ongoing project-related expenses – including ongoing costs of supporting the project deliverables once the project is completed. Ongoing expenses can include maintenance and labor expense.
- Depreciation – the depreciation (or write-off) of capital expenses over time.
- Amortization – the amortization (or write-off) of expenses related to the purchase of software.
- Benefits/Revenue – this category includes any increase in revenues or decrease in expenses that are derived from the completion of the project.

The lifecycle budget is often fed back into the Business Case where financial analysis can be completed.

If you are responsible for creating a project budget or lifecycle budget, make sure you work with someone with a financial background to validate your approach.

Technique: Tracking Actual Project Costs

Make sure that you establish the project budget in a way that makes the budget easy to track, by deliverable, reporting period or project phase.

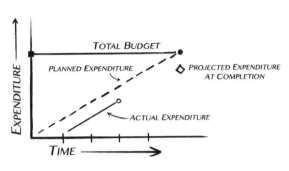

Using the budget we created in the "Developing the Project Budget" technique, a chart can be set up to graph the planned and actual project expenditures.

If, at the end of one month, the planned budget is $85,000 and the actual expenditure is $50,000, then the project is under budget at this point in time. As the Project Manager, you should take this information and determine:

- The reasons that the actual expenditure is below the planned expenditure. It could be that:
  - Expenses are less than planned (for example: lower labor or material costs)
  - Less work is completed than planned
- The estimated expenditure at project completion. Based on where the project is today and the remaining work, where do you project the project budget will be at the end of the project?

If you learn while tracking actuals that the projections at completion are different than planned, this should trigger a conversation with the Sponsor and Key Stakeholders. The purpose of this conversation is to determine if the new projections impact the Business Case and the financial justification of the project. It is acceptable to cancel or re-plan a project when projections after the project begins redefine what it will take to complete the project.

When tracking the project budget, remember that it is only one component of the project. Tracking the project timing and deliverable completion should be considered when analyzing project costs.

Technique: Utilizing Earned Value Management

Earned Value or Earned Value Management (EVM) is a standard set of equations used to determine project status at a point in time and create projections of project completion. EVM equations compare the planned work with the work actually performed to determine the schedule variance and the planned cost of the work completed against the actual expenditure to determine the cost variance.

Trends in work completion and financial expenditures can be determined by looking at the ratio between the planned and actual work and the planned and actual costs.

EVM is an advanced concept that is applied in organizations that have a high maturity in project management and access to detailed planning and tracking data at the appropriate level of granularity. Because EVM is not used in most organizations, the detailed equations will not be covered in this book. To learn more about EVM equations, a standard source is *A Guide to the Project Management Body of Knowledge* published by Project Management Institute.

Financing Summary

Defining project financials will help to answer:

- What needs to be bought?
- What will the project cost?

When making a buy or build decision, take the following items into consideration:

- Project time commitment – will buying or building support the project timing?
- Project cost – will buying or building support the project budget?
- Deliverable requirements – which approach will more likely deliver to the level of quality defined by the Sponsor and Key Stakeholders, buying or building?
- Resource availability and skills – do the resources available have the time and the skills necessary to build the deliverables to the requirements within the schedule defined for the project?

There are two types of budgets:

- Project Budget – includes all the costs associated with achieving a project goal. Budget categories include: labor, materials, consulting/vendor, travel, training, equipment, facilities and software.
- Lifecycle Budget – includes the project budget as well as ongoing costs and revenue generated by the project. The lifecycle budget includes: one-time project costs, ongoing project-related expenses, depreciation and amortization—the amortization and benefits/revenue.

If you are responsible for creating a project budget or lifecycle budget, make sure you work with someone with a financial background to validate your approach.

When tracking the project budget, remember that it is only one component of the project. Tracking the project timing and deliverable completion should be considered when analyzing project costs.

"Price is what you pay, value is what you get."
~Warren Buffett, American business magnate

Chapter 14: Project Execution

> *"Execution is everything."*
> ~Jeff Bridges, American actor, country musician and producer

Once the Project Plan is drafted, and the project gains approval to move to Execution, there is still a lot of work for the Project Manager. Most of the work involves keeping active watch of Key Stakeholders, working closely with the Sponsor, and motivating and leading the project team while capturing project actuals and comparing them to the baseline set up at the end of project planning. All of these topics where covered in Chapters 3–13 of this text.

The questions answered during Execution are:

- How will issues and requests for changes be managed?
- Is the project:
  - On time?
  - On budget?
  - Delivering the project scope?

This chapter introduces new topics and techniques for managing project issues and scope changes, and provides a summary of techniques for tracking project progress.

Technique: Managing Issues

Once you have a Project Plan approved and in place, project Execution can begin. During Execution, two events are likely to occur: the project will run into issues and you will be asked to change the scope of the project. This technique will focus on definitions, management strategies, and roles and responsibilities for issues (scope changes will be covered in the next technique).

Let's begin with a definition of the term issue: an issue is any event that has happened or is about to happen that will impact the project. Issues are referred to as the "known knowns"; they are the events we know that we know about. Issues are different from "known unknowns," which are the things we know we don't know about—otherwise, called risks. If this sounds confusing, it is not meant to be. Simply put, an issue has certainty and needs to be managed while risks have uncertainty (they may or may not occur, and need to be assessed).

Issue Management Lifecycle

Managing issues can be described by using a simple lifecycle. Issues, once identified, should be logged (or tracked so they are not forgotten), assigned to an individual for investigation, resolved and closed out. Let's look at each of these steps in more detail.

Identifying Issues – anyone can identify an issue. They are often identified by team members while working on the project.

Logging Issues – issues should be documented in a location accessible by all team members. Whether it is on a project website, shared drive or printed in a project binder, it should be stored in a central location for all to access. When logging an issue, be sure to include:

- Date the issue was first identified and documented.
- Description of the issue.
- Recommended Action to manage or resolve the issue.
- Name of the individual who identified, investigated or resolved the issue.
- Status of the issue: open, under investigation or resolved/closed.

For example:

Date	Description	Recommended Action	Name	Status	Closed Date
mm/ dd/yy	It is one week prior to training and few people have signed up	Sponsor to meet with Sales Manager	Project Manager	Closed	mm/dd/ yy

Date	Description	Recommended Action	Name	Status	Closed Date
mm/dd/yy	PMO guidelines and templates are out of date	Meet with Sponsor to get approval to use old documents, or for assistance in getting up-to-date templates	Team member	Open	mm/dd/yy

When deciding if an event should be logged as an issue, use these three questions as a guide. If you can answer yes to any of these questions, then document the event in the Issue Log:

1. Is there no known resolution?
2. Can you resolve the event, but others should be aware of the event?
3. Will the event impact the project?

Assigning Issues for Investigation – to ensure that issues don't get ignored, a specific individual who has both the skill to investigate and identify alternative resolutions and the authority to make decisions about the issue should be assigned responsibility for issue investigation.

Resolving Issues – most issues require a resolution. Some issues may require more effort to resolve than the impact of the issue. In this case, before an issue is resolved, it may be valuable to prioritize the issue. Issues can be prioritized by impact (on the project's ability to meet KPI) and effort (the labor and cost to resolve the issue):

Impact on Project	Effort to Resolve	Potential Action
High	High	This issue needs to be resolved; the team should invest time looking for alternative resolutions that have a lower impact on the project timing and budget
High	Low	This issue should be resolved and closed out quickly
Low	High	This issue could be set aside; you may be better off not resolving it
Low	Low	This issue should only be resolved if there is time without impacting the schedule, budget or project deliverable quality

Issue resolution should be documented in the Issue Log and integrated into the Project Plan. If the issue resolution causes a change to the approved project scope, then the issue resolution should be presented as a change and go through the scope change management process.

Closing Out Issues – once an issue resolution has been approved and the resolution has been integrated into the Project Plan, the issue can be closed out in the Issue Log.

Issue Management Roles and Responsibilities

Each project role has a unique responsibility when managing issues; the following are standard roles and responsibilities for issue management.

Project Role	Issue Management Responsibilities
  Project Manager	• Regular review of the Issue Log to ensure that issues are being managed proactively • Assign new issues to the appropriate individual for investigation and identifying alternative resolutions • Approve/reject issue resolutions • Move issue resolutions that will be scope changes to the Change Log and follow the scope change process • Integrate approved issue resolutions into the Project Plan
  Entire Project Team	• Active engagement in the issue management process • Identify issues • Log the issues they identify • Investigate the issue and identify alternative resolutions

Technique: Managing Scope Changes

A scope change is any modification to the scope documented and agreed to in the approved Project Plan. The best approach to managing scope is to begin with a clearly defined project scope statement. Many

> *"There is nothing permanent except change."*
> ~Heraclitus, Greek philosopher

projects have ambiguous goals (goals not meeting the SMART criteria), undefined deliverables (leaving much room for individual assumptions of what will and will not be created) and undocumented requirements for the defined deliverables (no common understanding of what the quality of delivers will be upon completion). Having a clearly defined project scope gives you a common baseline in which to begin all scope change conversations. The second element of scope change management that should be established early in project

---

Scope Change

Just to be extra clear in terminology: If you only talk about change, some people might think that you are talking about the changes that need to be made in the organization (organizational change management) to accept the project outcome. When adding the term scope in front of the word change, communication is clearer.

Planning is the level of authority each project role has in approving or rejecting a requested change.

 Scope changes can include: adding or changing deliverables; modifying (usually increasing) the features, functions and requirements to previously defined deliverables; providing the deliverables to a different or wider audience (which increases the work required); reducing the timing or funding of the project.

Scope Change Lifecycle

Scope change can also be described by using a simple lifecycle. Scope changes, once identified, should be logged, assigned to an individual for investigation, presented to the decision maker and closed out. Let's look at each of these steps in more detail.

Identifying Scope Changes – anyone can identify a potential change for a project. Changes are often identified by stakeholders during the life of the project as they gain a better understanding of what will be delivered.

Logging Scope Changes – change requests should be documented in a location accessible by all team members. When logging a change request, be sure to include:

- Date the scope change request was first identified and documented.
- Description of the requested scope change.
- Impact of *Accepting* the Change on the project work, staffing, timing, budget and value delivered, plus the impact on other work.
- Impact of *Rejecting* the Change on the project work, staffing, timing, budget and value delivered.
- Alternative Options or trade-offs that can be made to include the change (and remove something else from the project) that will not impact the timing or budget of the project.
- Name of the individual who requested the scope change.
- Status of the scope change: under investigation, approved, rejected.

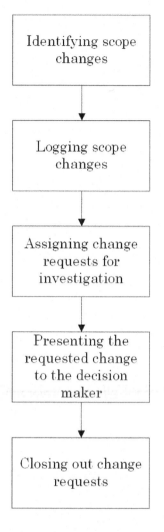

For example:

Date	Description	Impact of Accepting Change	Impact of Rejecting Change	Alternative Options	Name	Status
mm/ dd/ yy	The Sales Staff is not the only Sponsor within the organization; the training should be rolled out to a wider audience	Need to expand interviews and validate the Sponsor behaviors are standard across all types of projects; training will need to be updated and more training dates will need to be scheduled – additional cost is $12,000 and a one-month delay in project completion	Only the Sales Staff will be educated in their Sponsor role	Assume that the training for the Sales Staff does not need any modifications and just invite more people to attend training	PMO	Alternative option approved

Assigning Change Requests for Investigation – to ensure that scope change requests are properly investigated, a specific individual who has the skill to investigate and identify alternative resolutions about the requested change should be assigned responsibility for investigation. There are three different perspectives to consider when investigating a change request:

1. What is the impact of *accepting* the change on the project's time, cost, resources and quality, as well as the impact the requested change might have on other work currently in process? Scope changes are not free. They will consume time, resources and money. It is important to understand the total cost of the requested change so that the decision maker has the information necessary to make an informed decision.

2. What is the impact of *rejecting* the change on the project's time, cost, resources and quality? Sometimes rejecting a change request will result in a project delivering lower quality or performance than originally thought.

3. What alternatives exist to absorb the change without affecting time or cost? Sometimes, thinking creatively, there are trade-offs that exist (accept the requested change but eliminate something else from the project scope). It is worth identifying potential trade-offs when investigating a change request.

Not all changes have the same priority when it is time to investigate the change request. Use the following table to determine the priority of the change and what action you should take:

Time Required to Investigate Change Request	Impact on Project Value	Recommended Action
High	Low	Close out the change request without investigation
High	High	Discuss the need for the change, and determine if the interest in the change and the impact on value are worth diverting other project work to investigate
Low	Low	Bundle with other changes or close out the change
Low	High	Investigate the change request quickly

Presenting the Requested Change to the Decision Maker – the illustration used in this text for scope is a fence with a gate. The fence is to clearly define what is in scope, and the gate is to provide someone with the authority to add or remove items from the project scope. Defining who has the authority to make a decision on a change request should be established in the Planning stage. Change decisions include:

- Accepting the requested change and the impact on the project's time, cost and resource requirements.
- Rejecting (saying no to) the requested change.
- Deferring the requested change until later in the project. Deferring is saying yes, but deferring the implementation of the change until later in the project. For example: accepting the change, but not implementing the change until phase II of the project.

Changes can be:

- Bundled for investigation then presented as a collection for a decision.
- Quickly investigated and presented individually for a decision.

Closing Out Change Requests – once a change is investigated and a decision is made, the request can be closed out in the Change Log.

Scope Change Roles and Responsibilities

Each project role has unique responsibilities when managing changes; here are standard roles and responsibilities for change management.

Project Role	Scope Change Responsibilities
Sponsor	• Identifies potential scope changes, and presents them to the team member or Project Manager for investigation • Holds final authority to accept, reject or defer change requests
Stakeholders	• Identify potential scope changes, and presents them to the team member or Project Manager for investigation

Project Role	Scope Change Responsibilities
Project Manager	• Identifies potential changes • Manages the Change Log (ensuring that requested changes are investigated and that decisions are being made in a timely manner) • Holds authority within the predefined boundaries of the project to accept, reject of defer change requests • Presents requested change options to the appropriate decision maker
Project Team	• Identifies potential changes • Logs requested changes • Investigates the impact of the requested change • May have limited authority to accept, reject or defer a scope change if the change is minor and within the scope of their responsibility (a team member can make a change decision on work they are responsible for if it does not impact the time, cost or quality of the deliverable they are working on) • Implements approved scope changes

Technique: Tracking Progress During Execution

The point of monitoring or tracking progress during project Execution is to:

- Analyze progress in relationship to the plan
- Assess the ability of the project to achieve the project goal
- Make adjustments to the plan based on current progress
- Keep everyone aware of progress to date
- Produce an early warning of how the project is progressing according to the Project Plan

When tracking progress, make sure
that you compare data related to:

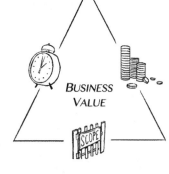

- Time – the amount of work
  actually completed compared
  to the amount of work scheduled for completion
- Cost – the amount of funds
  actually consumed compared
  to the amount of funds scheduled to be spent
- Scope – the deliverables created compared to what was
  planned, as well as the actual quality of each deliverable
  compared to the planned quality defined in the deliverable
  requirements

For each of these comparisons, it is critical to understand progress:

- At a point in time – where the project currently is compared
  to the Project Plan
- Projections at completion – based on the current assessment,
  where the project is projected to be at completion

These two data points (point in time and projections at completion)
are critical because, whether a project is ahead or behind at a point in
time, it may be more or less relevant if the projections at completion
are acceptable.

For more information on:

- Tracking Quality – review
  the technique for Monitoring
  Quality Progress in Chapter 7
- Tracking Financials – review
  the technique for Tracking

Actual Project Costs in Chapter 13
- Tracking Time – review the technique for Tracking the Schedule in Chapter 11
- Reporting Status – review the technique for Developing Status Reports in Chapter 12

Project Execution Summary

Once the project planning is completed and approved, the work of project execution begins. At this point in the project, there is still a lot of work for the Project Manager to do. As intensive as planning is, execution can

take up all of the Project Manager's time as they continue to apply the techniques of planning while managing issues and scope changes, tracking and communicating project progress, and providing leadership to the team. Some of the most important things the Project Manager should be focusing on during Execution are:

- Managing issues and scope changes by using the lifecycles provided in this chapter, and tracking them in a log, ensuring that each are documented and resolved appropriately.
- Making sure that everyone is aware of their individual project responsibilities.
- Tracking project progress against all sides of the project constraints: time, cost and scope. It is important to know if your project is on time and on budget but not delivering the value detailed in the project scope, or if you are delivering the scope on time but way over budget.

- Communicating proactively so that there are no surprises on the actual events that occur during Execution.
- Creating status reports based on the information needs of your Key Stakeholders.

"Plan your work for today and every day, then work your plan."
~Margaret Thatcher, Prime Minister
of the United Kingdom

Section 2: Summary

The techniques where presented to aid you in your project management application. The purpose of any technique is to speed up your ability to get work done in a standardized, repeatable and complete manner. Not all techniques are necessary on every project; and like anything, the more you understand it, and the more practice you have, the quicker it will help you get the job done.

When reviewing each technique, challenge yourself to understand the purpose of the technique and when to apply it on your project. Obviously, you can apply necessary techniques in the Planning stage and then continue ongoing planning during Execution; but know that it is not too late in Execution to apply any of these techniques for the first time.

See Appendix B for a summary of project management topics and techniques, and the questions they help answer.

APPENDIXES

The appendixes contain summary information in a quick reference format, including:

- A project management summary

- Summary of techniques and the questions they answer

- Information on how this text maps to the Project Management Institute's PMBOK

- Samples of the project management deliverables shared in the text

- A list of recommended collaborative planning workshops

- Recommendations of how this text can be used in the classroom

- Recommended reading

Appendix A: Project Management Summary

The following is a quick overview of the key concepts in project management.

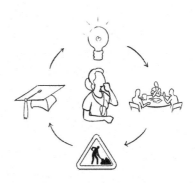

Initiation – Start with an idea that is briefly documented in a Project Charter (business need, Key Stakeholders, preliminary scope—project goal and high-level deliverables—high-level risk, timing, cost and key resources). The Charter document should be created collaboratively between the Project Manager and the Sponsor. If you secure agreement to the high-level estimates in the Charter, work with the Sponsor to provide the resources necessary for project planning.

Planning – Through a collaborative effort:

- Identify Key Stakeholders and their success criteria
- Reflect on past projects to leverage lessons learned
- Clarify the project goal, and verify that the project is aligned with the organization's strategy and delivers value
- Define the final, interim and project management deliverables necessary to achieve the project goal
- For each deliverable, define the:
  - Requirements they must meet to satisfy Key Stakeholder success criteria

- o Work, effort and resources necessary to build each deliverable
- Identify, assess and develop a strategy for project risks; and embed the mitigation (proactive) risk management strategies into the project scope
- Clearly define project roles and responsibilities while building a positive team experience
- Determine the budget by adding up the costs associated with developing each deliverable
- Determine the schedule by sequencing, across the calendar, all the project deliverables
- Create a communication plan to ensure that everyone has the information they need to understand and support the project

Document all the above in a Project Plan, and reconfirm organizational commitment to support project execution.

Execution – During the Execution stage, track the project actuals in comparison to the Project Plan. Manage issues and follow any policies to ensure that the right individuals are making informed decisions about accepting or rejecting potential project changes. Continue attending to team dynamics and on-boarding new individuals to the project. Monitor deliverable completion against their requirements, ensuring that the level of quality delivered is sufficient to meet stakeholder needs. Revisit the Planning stage as necessary— clarifying work; evaluating risks; and reestimating time, cost and resources as more information becomes available. Ensure that the communication plan is executed and that feedback is being captured.

Closing – Once the project deliverables are complete and accepted by the Sponsor (or the project is canceled), move the project into the Closing stage. Use this stage to reflect on value delivered and project achievements, capture lessons learned, celebrate success and close out any project documentation.

Congratulations on your application of project management! I hope it drives your project success.

Appendix B: Project Management Topics and Standard Techniques

This appendix is meant to be a quick reference for you to utilize to ensure you are asking the right questions and gathering the necessary information to successfully plan and execute your project. The following is a list of each project management topic and the questions they help answer, as well as the techniques that can be used to answer the questions.

Topic	Questions	Techniques
Goals Chapter 3	• What will the project achieve? • What does success look like? • How will we know when we are done?	• Creating SMART goals

Topic	Questions	Techniques
Stakeholders Chapter 4	• Who will be impacted? • What are their expectations? • How engaged are they in the project? • How important are they to the project? • How does the project satisfy their needs?	• Providing role clarity • Identifying Stakeholders • Assessing Stakeholder engagement • Determining Stakeholder perceptions • Developing Stakeholder Management Strategies
Knowledge Chapter5	• What do you already know that will help drive project success? • What have you learned that will drive future success?	• Leveraging past learning • Capturing current learning
Deliverables Chapter 6	• What needs to be built/created/delivered: ○ At the end of the project? ○ During the life of the project? ○ To manage the project?	• Identifying deliverables • Creating a Work Breakdown Structure (WBS) or Decomposition Diagram

Topic	Questions	Techniques
Quality Chapter 7	• How will you ensure that the project deliverables will meet Stakeholder expectations?	• Defining quality requirements • Prioritizing requirements • Monitoring quality progress
Work Chapter 8	• What work needs to be done? • How long will the work take? • What skills are needed? • How many resources (people, materials, facilities) do you need to complete the work?	• Developing work packages • Estimating effort and duration
Project Team Chapter 9	• Does everyone understand their project role? • How will you build a positive team?	• Defining roles and responsibilities • On-boarding the team • Selecting a team structure • Building and developing the team • Motivating the team with rewards and recognition • Encouraging positive conflict

Topic	Questions	Techniques
Risks Chapter 10	• How much uncertainty is okay? • How will uncertainty be handled?	• Identifying risks • Assessing risks • Creating risk management strategies
Timing Chapter 11	• How long will the project take?	• Sequencing work • Developing a short-interval schedule • Establishing contingency • Tracking the schedule
Communication Chapter 12	• Who needs information on the project? • What do they need to know? • When do they need information? • How will they get the information?	• Building the communication plan • Developing status reports • Scheduling team meetings
Financing Chapter 13	• What needs to be purchased? • What will the project cost?	• Making a buy or build decision • Establishing a project budget • Developing a lifecycle budget • Tracking actual project costs • Utilizing Earned Value Management

Topic	Questions	Techniques

Project Execution
 	
Chapter 14
	• How will issues and changes be managed?
	• Is the project:
	   o On time?
	   o On budget?
	   o Delivering the project scope?
		• Managing issues
		• Managing scope changes
		• Tracking progress during Execution

Appendix C: Mapping this Text to PMI's PMBOK

If the title of this appendix sounds like a foreign language to you, then maybe you can skip this information. If, on the other hand, you know what the Project Management Institute (PMI) is and are familiar with the *Project Management Body of Knowledge* (PMBOK) published by PMI, then the brief time it will take to read this will help you reconcile how the techniques and concepts in this text are mapped to the PMBOK.

The intent of the text is to complement the good work of PMI by providing a simple application-based approach to applying the project management techniques and best practices that I have found helpful in my twenty-plus years of consulting.

Let's look at the current PMBOK areas of focus and where those concepts are covered in the text:

PMBOK Knowledge Area	Related Text Chapters
Scope Management	Chapter 3: Goals
	Chapter 6: Deliverables
	Chapter 7: Quality
	Chapter 8: Work
Communications	Chapter 12: Communication
Stakeholders	Chapter 4: Stakeholders
Risk	Chapter 10: Risks
Time	Chapter 11: Timing

PMBOK Knowledge Area	Related Text Chapters
Cost	Chapter 13: Financing
Human Resources	Chapter 9: Project Team
Quality	Chapter 7: Quality
Integration	Chapter 14: Project Execution Chapter 5: Knowledge

Appendix D: Sample Project Plan

This appendix contains the Project Plan for our sample project, which was built by using the techniques presented in Chapters 3–13.

Scope:

Goal – Provide project management training to the entire sales staff, so that the sales team can execute their role as Project Sponsors by end of first quarter 20xx.

Work Breakdown Structure:

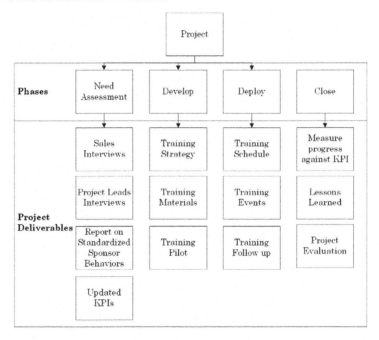

Deliverables and Acceptance Criteria:

Deliverable Type	Deliverable	Acceptance Criteria
Project Final	Training Events	Meets Sales Managers' timing expectations Drives standardized behavior for Sponsors
	Measure of progress against KPI	Meets Key Stakeholders KPI with pre- and post-project metrics
Project Interim	Sales interviews	At least five interviews Captures issues and success criteria from Sales
	Project Leads interviews	At least five interviews Captures issues and meets Project Lead's success criteria
	Report on standard Sponsor behaviors	Summary report of interviews Provide a half-hour PowerPoint presentation to Sales Managers and PMO
	Updated KPI	Based on results of interview report Must be quantifiable and have current metrics
	Training Strategy	Meets KPIs Approved by Sales Managers and includes training best practices
	Training Materials	Job aids Participant materials Slides Pre and post work Supports training strategy
	Training Pilot	Pilot training must have a minimum of two participants from Sales and two participants from Project Leads
	Training Schedule	Multiple offerings in multiple locations
	Training Follow Up	Based on training strategy

Deliverable Type	Deliverable	Acceptance Criteria
Project Management	Project Plan	Follows PMO standards
	Project Evaluation	Follows PMO standards
	Status Reports	Follows PMO standards Progress against KPI

Risk Management Strategy:

Date	Risk	Assessment	Mitigation	Responsible for Mitigation	Contingency
mm/ dd/ yy	Conflicting KPIs between Project Leads and Sales Staff	High	Identify industry best practice KPIs for Sponsors, and use that as a discussion point during the Project Leads and Sponsor interviews	Training (Project Manager)	Work with PMO and Sales Managers to have them establish common KPI
mm/ dd/ yy	Low attendance in training by Sales Staff	High	Engage Sales Managers in training strategy development so they support the project	Training (Project Manager)	Work with PMO to gain Sales Managers' support

Date	Risk	Assessment	Mitigation	Responsible for Mitigation	Contingency
mm/ dd/ yy	May not get the right mix of people in the pilot	Medium	-	-	Reschedule pilot or find back-up participants
mm/ dd/ yy	Low attendance in training by Project Leads	Low	-	-	-

Project Team's Responsibilities by Deliverable:

Deliverable-Based RACI	Project Team				
Deliverables	Sponsor	Training (Project Manager)	Sales Staff	Sales Managers	Project Leads
Training Events	I	A, R	R	I	R
Measure of progress against KPI	I	A, R	C	C	I
Sales interviews		A,R	R	I	I
Project Leads interviews		A,R			R
Report on standard Sponsor behaviors	R	A,R	I	I	I
Updated KPI	I	A,R		I	I
Training Strategy	I	A,R		C	
Training Materials		A,R			
Training Pilot		A,R	I	C	C
Training Schedule	I	A,R	I		I

Training Follow Up		A,R	I	C	C
Project Plan	A	R			
Project Evaluation	A	R	C	C	C
Status Reports	I	A,R	I	I	I

Stakeholder Management Strategy:

Stakeholder	KPI	Strategy to Maximize Engagement
Project Leads	Consistant behavior from active supporting Sponsors	Have Project Leads attend training to understand Sponsor behavior expectations Interview Project Leads prior to training development to understand their needs
Training	Meeting project time, cost and performance requirements	Already fully engaged
Sales Staff	?	Interview selected Sales Staff to understand their needs and KPIs Utilize Sales Managers to drive up Sales Staff's engagement
Sales Managers	Minimum disturbance to Sales daily work	Work with Sales Managers to design a training approach that they will support
PMO	Meeting project time, cost and performance requirements	Provide status and follow PMO project guidelines

Communication Plan:

Audience (Who)	Content (What)	Timing (When)	Medium (How)	Responsible	Feedback
Project Managers, Sales Staff and Sales Managers	Need for training	At project kick-off	Face to face	PMO (Sponsor)	Commitment to attend training
	Interview schedule	At project kick-off	Face to face	Training (Project Manager)	Accept interview meeting notice
	Defined Sponsor Behaviors	Post interviews	Webinar	PMO (Sponsor) and Training (Project Manager)	-
	Follow-up sessions	At training	Face to face	Training (Project Manager)	Attendance
	Project Evaluation	At project completion	Webinar	Training (Project Manager)	-
	Training schedule	At project kick-off	E-mail	Training (Project Manager)	Accept training notification
PMO	Project Plan	mm/dd/yy	Face to face	Training (Project Manager)	Approval
	Training Plan	mm/dd/yy	Face to face	Training (Project Manager)	Approval
	Status	Every other week	E-mail	Training (Project Manager)	-
	Project Evaluation	At project completion	Webinar	Training (Project Manager)	-

Deliverable-Based Gantt Chart (Schedule):

ID	Deliverables	January		February				March			
		1/19	1/26	2/2	2/9	2/16	2/23	3/2	3/9	3/16	3/23
1	Project Plan	■									
2	Training Events								■		
3	Measure of progress against KPI	■									
4	Sales interviews	■	■								
5	Project Leads interviews	■	■								
6	Report on standard Sponsor behaviors				■						
7	Updated KPI			■							
8	Training Strategy				■						
9	Training Materials					■	■				
10	Training Pilot							■			
11	Training Schedule					■					
12	Training Follow up									■	
13	Project Evaluation									■	
14	Status Reports			■	■	■	■				

Budget:

Budget Category	Expense
Labor	50,000
Materials	500
Travel	5,000
Facilities and Food	2,500
Total	**58,000**

Appendix E:
Workshop Ideas

Over the years, my favor-
ite approach to planning has
remained the same: facilitating
collaborative workshops that
include representation from the
business and project team.

Collaborative workshops provide a way for the entire team to create a common agreement and vision for the project. This appendix
provides a list of all the recommended workshops. Not all workshop
ideas need to be used for every project. Review the list of workshops
topics and select the ones that will benefit your current project.

- Holding a Project Planning Workshop (Chapter 2, page 30)
- Establishing Common Project Goals (Chapter 3, page 60)
- Stakeholder Identification and Prioritization (Chapter 4, page 69)
- Defining Stakeholder Engagement (Chapter 4, page 74)
- Developing a Stakeholder Management Strategy (Chapter 4, page 82)
- Gathering Best Practices for the Project (Chapter 5, page 89)
- Capturing Lessons Learned for Future Projects (Chapter 5, page 92)
- Defining Project Deliverables (Chapter 6, page 100)
- Defining Deliverable Quality (Chapter 7, page 110)

- Developing Work Packages (Chapter 8, page 118)
- Establishing Clear Roles and Responsibilities (Chapter 9, page 131)
- Defining Project Risk Tolerance (Chapter 10, page 148)
- Managing Project Risks (Chapter 10, page 157)
- Creating the Project Schedule (Chapter 11, page 170)
- Developing a Communication Plan (Chapter 12, page 187)
- Establishing a Project Budget (Chapter 13, page 199)
- Holding a Project Closing Workshop (Chapter 2, page 47)

Appendix F: How to Use this Book in a Classroom

This book was designed to assist anyone in their pursuit of project management best practices. As the book was being written, I used it as supplemental reading and finally as the text for undergraduate project management classes.

Understanding project management is like getting your MBA. There is a lot of information from many different disciplines to master. How this material is covered in the classroom is dependent on the experience of the students and the level of knowledge you would like them to leave with at the end of the course. Each topic listed below can be covered at a high-level during a traditional college week (assuming about 2 ¾ hours of classroom time a week). Many topics could be expanded to cover a complete semester. I recommend that you take a week to cover the topics for which students need to gain awareness. More than one week will be necessary for topics where the students need to build skills or you wish to utilize the potential activities.

As part of the semester, the class is divided into working teams; each team picks a project and develops an entire Project Plan to present at the end of the semester. Sometimes, I provide classroom time to work on their team projects. I do weekly mini-quizzes, which cover the previous week's topic, in place of a mid-term.

Here is more detail on each topic with potential activities and assignments to complete in the classroom or as homework.

For my class, I used the following syllabus:

Week	Topic	Reading
1	Introductions and expectations Project Management Overview	Chapters 1 and 2
2	Defining project success – Goals and Stakeholders	Chapters 3 and 4
3	Knowledge	Chapter 5
4	Project Scope	Chapters 6, 7 and 8
5 and 6	Project Team	Chapter 9
7	Risk Management	Chapter 10
8	Classroom time to begin work on team projects	
9	Communication	Chapter 12
10 and 11	Scheduling – Microsoft Project	Chapter 11
12	Financing	Chapter 13
13	Project Execution	Chapter 14
14	Team project practice presentation	
15	Team project final presentation	
16	Final	

Topic	Project Management Overview
Key Learning	What is project management? Lifecycle, key roles and project management deliverables
Reading	Chapters 1 and 2
Potential Activities and Assignments	<ul><li>Read the Standish Group's Chaos Report on the success and challenges in applying project management</li><li>Identifying project management applications in your discipline (e.g., IT, construction, finance)</li><li>Look for examples of PMOs and the services they provide</li><li>Learn about project management certifications from PMI and Prince2</li><li>Look for job postings and qualifications for project managers</li></ul>

Topic	Defining Project Success
Key Learning	Establishing project goals and identifying Key Stakeholders
Reading	Chapters 3 and 4
Potential Activities and Assignments	<ul><li>Practice taking ambiguous goals and reframing them as SMART goals</li><li>Look up KPIs by industry</li><li>Challenge the class to determine how KPIs would be measured and tracked. See if you can find KPIs that can be tracked during the life of the project and not just at project completion</li><li>Find a case study and use the Workshop Ideas to identify, prioritize and determine engagement levels; and create a Stakeholder Management Strategy</li></ul>

Topic	Knowledge
Key Learning	Capturing knowledge from past projects
Reading	Chapter 5
Potential Activities and Assignments	• Provide examples of benchmarking and how past work can be used to improve future work • Complete role plays of individual interviews (maybe using past classes – what they learned, recommendations for new students, what they would do differently if they took the class again) • Set up a mock planning session, using the Workshop Idea to brainstorm lessons learned, and discuss how this information would be integrated into a Project Plan

Topic	Project Scope
Key Learning	Defining project deliverables, establishing deliverable quality and defining project work
Reading	Chapters 6, 7 and 8
Potential Activities and Assignments	• Review the SMART goals – they are part of scope • Create Work Breakdown Structures • Determine requirements for identified deliverables • Define the work for the deliverables • Discuss how the deliverables and work identified are usually greater than one might have thought before the project was scoped • Discuss how the defined scope should include the activities from the Stakeholder Management Strategy and deliver to Key Stakeholders' KPI

Topic	Project Team
Key Learning	Developing the project team
Reading	Chapter 9
Potential Activities and Assignments	• Take a personality assessment like DiSC, Myer-Briggs (or other free assessments available on the Internet). Discuss how different personalities impact the project team • Watch a video clip on stages of team development (many are available on youtube.com) • Use the Workshop Idea and apply it in the classroom • Add content on cultural differences in global teams and how that will impact team dynamics

Topic	Risk Management
Key Learning	Understanding risk tolerance and developing a risk management plan
Reading	Chapter 10
Potential Activities and Assignments	• Complete the risk tolerance questions and see how everyone's risk tolerance is unique – discuss how this can impact project planning • Use the Workshop Ideas and simulate the risk management technique • Discuss how the mitigation strategies will impact the project scope • Determine how much time and money should be held in buffer in case some risk contingency needs to be implemented

Topic	**Communication**
Key Learning	Establishing a project communication plan
Reading	Chapter 12
Potential Activities and Assignments	• Play a version of "telephone" to emphasis how communication breaks down • Develop a communication plan, using the Workshop Idea from the chapter • Discuss cultural differences in communications • Discuss how organizational level and role can impact communications • Design a status report that talks to project tracking and includes progress against KPIs • Talk about how roles, biases and perspectives impact the effectiveness of communications

Topic	**Scheduling**
Key Learning	Defining project dependencies and creating the project schedule
Reading	Chapter 11
Potential Activities and Assignments	• Apply the Workshop Idea to develop a schedule using the deliverables identified in the scoping activity • Add content on using the forward and backward passes to calculate critical path • Use Microsoft Project or other scheduling tool in a hands-on activity to create an electronic version of the project schedule • Look at Agile schedules and discuss the similarities and differences with traditional schedules

Topic	Financing
Key Learning	Developing the project budget and lifecycle costs of the project
Reading	Chapter 13
Potential Activities and Assignments	• Discuss Return on Investment (ROI), break-even and Net Present Value concepts used in lifecycle budgeting • Create a project and lifecycle budget for a project • Look at different budgeting templates (using the Internet)

Topic	Project Execution
Key Learning	Tracking project progress, and managing issues and changes
Reading	Chapter 14
Potential Activities and Assignments	• Review issue and scope change log examples from the Internet • Provide examples of issues for a project and have students determine if the resolution can be implemented or should be managed as a change • Identify potential changes and have students assess the impact of accepting or rejecting the change on the project

If you are interested in using this book for teaching in a university class, visit www.cectraining.com for access to presentation materials, activities and quizzes.

Appendix G:
Recommended Reading

There are many books on the subject of project management. The following is a list of a few that I have in my personal library. They can be a good starting point for anyone interested in more information on any of the topics covered in this book.

Drucker, Peter F. *Managing for Results*. Reissue ed. New York: HarperBusiness, 2006. Print.

Eckerson, Wayne W. *Performance Dashboards: Measuring, Monitoring, and Managing Your Business*. Second ed. Hoboken, NJ: John Wiley & Sons, 2010. Print.

Goldratt, Eliyahu M. *What Is This Thing Called Theory of Constraints and How Should It Be Implemented?* Great Barrington, MA: North River, 1990. Print.

Heath, Chip, and Dan Heath. *Made to Stick: Why Some Ideas Survive and Others Die*. New York: Random House, 2007. Print.

Katzenbach, Jon R., and Douglas K. Smith. *The Wisdom of Teams: Creating the High-Performance Organization (Collins Business Essentials)*. Reprint ed. New York: HarperBusiness, 2006. Print.

Kerzner, Harold, Ph.D. *Project Management: A Systems Approach to Planning, Scheduling, and Controlling*. Eleventh ed. Hoboken, NJ: John Wiley & Sons, 2013. Print.

———. *Project Management Metrics, KPIs, and Dashboards: A Guide to Measuring and Monitoring Project Performance*. Hoboken, NJ: John Wiley & Sons, 2011. Print.

————. *Using the Project Management Maturity Model: Strategic Planning for Project Management.* Second ed. Hoboken, NJ: John Wiley & Sons, 2005. Print.

Kerzner, Harold, Ph.D., and Frank P. Saladis, PMP. *What Executives Need to Know About Project Management.* Hoboken, NJ: John Wiley & Sons, 2009. Print.

Pande, Peter S., Robert P. Neuman, and Roland R. Cavanagh. *The Six Sigma Way: How GE, Motorola, and Other Top Companies Are Honing Their Performance.* New York: McGraw-Hill, 2000. Print.

Paulk, Mark C., Charles V. Weber, Bill Curtis, and Mary Beth Chrissis. *The Capability Maturity Model: Guidelines for Improving the Software Process.* Reading, MA: Addison-Wesley Pub., 1994. Print.

Glossary

This glossary focuses on key terms related to project management as well as other terms and abbreviations used within the text of this book.

aka. An abbreviation for *also known as*.

Business Case. The business justification for a project.

buffer. See **contingency**.

Capability Maturity Model Integration (CMMI). Software Engineering Institute's model that provides a standard for which many processes can be assessed.

change. See **scope change**.

Change Log. The log that is used to track requested changes (often referred to as scope change) to the project once the Project Plan has been approved.

Closing. The final step (phase or stage) of a project that is used to capture project learning and improve the strategies used in future projects.

CMMI. An abbreviation for *Capability Maturity Model Integration*. See also **Capability Maturity Model Integration (CMMI)**.

contingency. Also called *buffer* or *safety*. The additional time or money in a project used to absorb the things you did not know you did not know about (sometimes called the "unknown unknowns").

critical path. The longest chain of work sequenced by dependences.

Decomposition Diagram. See **Work Breakdown Structure (WBS)**.

deliverables. Something tangible that is created as a result of the project. See also **project deliverables** and **project management deliverables**.

duration. The total time to complete the work, taking into consideration the effort, calendar days plus the availability of resources (e.g., eight hours of effort for a person who is working only 20 percent of the time on the project will take a duration of five days).

Earned Value or Earned Value Management (EVM). A standard set of equations used to determine project status at a point in time and create projections of project completion.

effort. The amount of time it takes to complete the work without the consideration of the calendar.

EVM. An abbreviation for *Earned Value Management.* See also **Earned Value or Earned Value Management (EVM)**.

Execution. The third step (stage or phase) of a project—when the project work is done.

float. Also called *slack.* The work items or deliverables that are not on the critical path.

Gantt chart. The graphical representation of a project schedule that displays deliverables or major blocks of work across time.

Gatekeeper. A project decision maker.

Initiation. The first step (phase or stage) of a project that is used to clarify what the idea is, and develop a high-level best guess of what work, resources and time it will take to bring the idea to reality.

issue. Any event that has happened or is about to happen that will impact the project. Issues are referred to as the "known knowns."

Issue Log. The log that is used to track events that occur and require action during project execution.

IT. An abbreviation for *information technology.*

Key Performance Indicator. A specific expectation or success criteria for the outcome of a project.

Key Stakeholder. The high-priority stakeholders—the ones that usually have more interest in the project execution or project outcome, more influence on the work being done, and/or more power and authority within the organization. See also **Stakeholder**.

KPI. An abbreviation for *Key Performance Indicator.* See also **Key Performance Indicator**.

Lessons Learned. The document that captures the knowledge acquired during the project from the perspectives of the Sponsor, Stakeholders, Project Manager and project team members.

milestone. A point in time on a project schedule that indicates when a specific event will occur.

MoSCoW. The technique for prioritizing requirements into: must have, should have, could have and won't have.

Network Diagram. Also called *Program Evaluation Review Technique (PERT)*. A visual display of either project deliverables or project work organized by finish-to-start dependency.

PERT. An abbreviation for *Program Evaluation Review Technique*. See also **Network Diagram**.

Planning. The second step (phase or stage) of a project that is used to create the detailed strategy needed to achieve the approved project goals.

PMBOK. An abbreviation for *Project Management Body of Knowledge*. See also ***Project Management Body of Knowledge (PMBOK)***.

PMI. An abbreviation for *Project Management Institute*.

PMO. An abbreviation for *Project (or Program) Management Office*. See also **Project (or Program) Management Office**.

Program Evaluation Review Technique (PERT). See **Network Diagram**.

project. Something new or something unique that needs to get done.

Project Charter. A project management deliverable that documents the common understanding of a project need and high-level project strategy. See also **project management deliverables**.

project deliverables. Items created to achieve the project goals. See also **project management deliverables**.

Project Evaluation. A project management deliverable that provides an overall summary of the project, assesses the project's actual performance versus the planned performance, and highlights key improvements that can be leveraged for future projects.

project management. Standardized tools and techniques that increase the likelihood a project will be planned and executed successfully.

Project Management Body of Knowledge (PMBOK). The standard for project management, published by Project Management Institute.

project management deliverables. Items created for the management of a formal project. See also **project deliverables**.

project management maturity. An assessment within an organization that measures the acceptance and use of a standardized project management process.

Project Manager. The person responsible for facilitating the project planning, execution and closing while providing leadership to the project team.

Project (or Program) Management Office. A function within an organization that is dedicated to the support of project management.

Project Plan. Also called *Statement of Work (SOW)*. An evergreen project management deliverable that contains a detailed project strategy.

project team. The personnel who support the Project Manager and complete the project work.

R&D. An abbreviation for *research and development*.

RACI. A chart that is used to define project responsibilities by deliverable: Responsible (doer of the work), Accountable (ensures that the work gets done), Consult (has knowledge or information that needs to be included in the creation of the deliverable), Inform (needs information about the status or completion of the deliverable).

requirements. The expectations of the project, which are often defined in terms of features, functions or value delivered.

residual risk. The amount of remaining risk after high risks have been mitigated.

risk. The uncertainty that could impact the outcome of a project.

risk reserve. A buffer of time and money held in reserve to absorb a portion of the risk contingency if the risk occurs and the contingency plan needs to be executed.

risk tolerance. The amount of risk that is appropriate for the project.

risk trigger. An early indicator that a risk is about to occur.

ROI. An abbreviation for *return on investment.*

ROM. An abbreviation for *Rough Order of Magnitude.* See also **Rough Order of Magnitude (ROM).**

Rough Order of Magnitude (ROM). A high-level estimate that is used to determine the amount of effort and duration required for a project.

safety. See **contingency.**

scope. The term used to define what will and will not be included in the project; scope includes: goals, deliverables, quality and work.

scope change. Any modification to the scope that is documented and agreed to in the approved Project Plan.

SDLC. An abbreviation for *software development lifecycle.*

SEI. An abbreviation for *Software Engineering Institute.*

slack. See **float.**

SME. An abbreviation for *Subject Matter Expert.* See also **Subject Matter Expert (SME).**

SOW. An abbreviation for *Statement of Work.* See also **Project Plan.**

Sponsor. The person who represents the primary project benefactor and sets the overall project direction.

Stakeholder. Anyone who is actively involved in the project, or impacted by the execution or completion of the project. See also **Key Stakeholder.**

Statement of Work (SOW). See **Project Plan.**

Steering Committee. A team that provides a cross-functional perspective and overall support for project planning and execution.

Subject Matter Expert (SME). The person who provides expertise on project strategy and project-related information.

WBS. An abbreviation for *Work Breakdown Structure.* See also **Work Breakdown Structure (WBS).**

Work Breakdown Structure (WBS). A project management term used to reference breaking all the project work down in a hierarchical and structured or organized manner.

Work Package. A bundle of work that, once completed, creates a completed deliverable or portion of a deliverable.

workshop. A collaborative working meeting held for the purpose of creating a common vision and strategy to achieve the project goal.

CPSIA information can be obtained at www.ICGtesting.com
Printed in the USA
BVOW06s0402021015

420350BV00009B/202/P